OCEANS

How We Use the Seas

OUR FRAGILE PLANET

OCEANS

How We Use the Seas

DANA DESONIE, PH.D.

CHELSEA HOUSE
PUBLISHERS
An imprint of Infobase Publishing

Oceans

Copyright © 2008 by Dana Desonie, Ph.D.

Chelsea House
An imprint of Infobase Publishing
132 West 31st Street
New York NY 10001

Library of Congress Cataloging-in-Publication Data
Desonie, Dana.
    Oceans : how we use the seas / Dana Desonie.
        p. cm. — (Our fragile planet)
    Includes bibliographical references.
    ISBN-13: 978-0-8160-6216-4 (hardcover)
    ISBN-10: 0-8160-6216-1 (hardcover)
  1. Oceanography—Juvenile literature.   2. Ocean—Juvenile literature.   I. Title.   II. Series.

    GC21.5.D47 2007
    551.46—dc22

                                        2007013560

Chelsea House books are available at special discounts when purchased in bulk quantities for businesses, associations, institutions, or sales promotions. Please call our Special Sales Department in New York at (212) 967-8800 or (800) 322-8755.

You can find Chelsea House on the World Wide Web at http://www.chelseahouse.com

Text design by Annie O'Donnell
Cover design by Ben Peterson

Printed in the United States of America

Bang NMSG 10 9 8 7 6 5 4 3 2 1

This book is printed on acid-free paper.

All links and Web addresses were checked and verified to be correct at the time of publication. Because of the dynamic nature of the Web, some addresses and links may have changed since publication and may no longer be valid.

Cover photograph: © Simon Pederson / Shutterstock.com

Contents

Preface

The planet is a marvelous place: a place with blue skies, wild storms, deep lakes, and rich and diverse ecosystems. The tides ebb and flow, baby animals are born in the spring, and tropical rain forests harbor an astonishing array of life. The Earth sustains living things and provides humans with the resources to maintain a bountiful way of life: water, soil, and nutrients to grow food, and the mineral and energy resources to build and fuel modern society, among many other things.

The physical and biological sciences provide an understanding of the whys and hows of natural phenomena and processes—why the sky is blue and how metals form, for example—and insights into how the many parts are interrelated. Climate is a good example. Among the many influences on the Earth's climate are the circulation patterns of the atmosphere and the oceans, the abundance of plant life, the quantity of various gases in the atmosphere, and even the size and shapes of the continents. Clearly, to understand climate it is necessary to have a basic understanding of several scientific fields and to be aware of how these fields are interconnected.

As Earth scientists like to say, the only thing constant about our planet is change. From the ball of dust, gas, and rocks that came together 4.6 billion years ago to the lively and diverse globe that orbits the Sun today, very little about the Earth has remained the same for long. Yet, while change is fundamental, people have altered the environment unlike any other species in Earth's history. Everywhere there are reminders of our presence. A look at the sky might show a sooty cloud or a jet contrail. A look at the sea might reveal plastic refuse, oil, or only a few fish swimming where once they had been countless. The land has been deforested and strip-mined. Rivers and lakes have been polluted. Changing conditions and habitats have caused some plants and animals to expand their populations, while others have become extinct. Even the climate—which for millennia was thought to be beyond human influence—has been shifting due to alterations in the makeup of atmospheric gases brought about by human activities. The planet is changing fast and people are the primary cause.

OUR FRAGILE PLANET is a set of eight books that celebrate the wonders of the world by highlighting the scientific processes behind them. The books also look at the science underlying the tremendous influence humans are having on the environment. The set is divided into volumes based on the large domains on which humans have had an impact: *Atmosphere, Climate, Hydrosphere, Oceans, Geosphere, Biosphere,* and *Polar Regions.* The volume *Humans and the Natural Environment* describes the impact of human activity on the planet and explores ways in which we can conserve valuable natural resources.

A core belief expressed in each volume is that to mitigate the impacts humans are having on the Earth, each of us must understand the scientific processes that operate in the natural world. We must understand how human activities disrupt those processes and use that knowledge to predict ways that changes in one system will affect seemingly unrelated systems. These books express the belief that science is the solid ground from which we can reach an agreement on the behavioral changes that we must adopt—both as individuals and as a society—to solve the problems caused by the impact of humans on our fragile planet.

Acknowledgments

I would like to thank, above all, the scientists who have dedicated their lives to the study of the Earth, especially those engaged in the important work of understanding how human activities are impacting the planet. Many thanks to the staff of Facts On File and Chelsea House for their guidance and editing expertise: Frank Darmstadt, Executive Editor; Brian Belval, Senior Editor; and Leigh Ann Cobb, independent developmental editor. Dr. Tobi Zausner located the color images that illustrate our planet's incredible beauty and the harsh reality of the effects human activities are having on it. Thanks also to my agent, Jodie Rhodes, who got me involved in this project.

Family and friends were a great source of support and encouragement as I wrote these books. Special thanks to the May '97 Moms, who provided the virtual water cooler that kept me sane during long days of writing. Cathy Propper was always enthusiastic as I was writing the books, and even more so when they were completed. My mother, Irene Desonie, took great care of me as I wrote for much of June 2006. Mostly importantly, my husband, Miles Orchinik, kept things moving at home when I needed extra writing time and provided love, support, and encouragement when I needed that, too. This book is dedicated to our children, Reed and Maya, who were always loving, and usually patient. I hope these books do a small bit to help people understand how their actions impact the future for all children.

Introduction

Humans are land-centered. When we think of where resources come from or where environmental protections should be instituted, we think almost exclusively of the land that we inhabit. Yet, the oceans are the Earth's dominant surface feature, covering 71% of the planet's face. The dominance of surface water is why, when viewed from elsewhere in the solar system, the Earth looks like a blue dot. Besides being vast, the oceans are also deep, about 13,000 feet (4,000 m) on average. Their vastness, depth, and darkness make the oceans one of the great unknowns.

Of course, people do know and love the sea, but most only experience it from the shore or from a boat on its surface. Very few are able to venture deeper into the ocean than the 150 feet (45 m) a scuba diver can descend, a mere eyelash compared with the ocean's depth. Scientists explore the seas using sophisticated technologies and then disperse the knowledge they gather to the public. This body of information helps people to appreciate the oceans, to understand how ocean systems operate, and to devise plans for their protection.

Without its oceans, the Earth would be a very different planet. The seas play a major role in the water cycle: They store a tremendous amount of water and provide a large surface from which water can evaporate into the atmosphere. The oceans receive water as rain or from rivers and streams that flow across the planet's surface. Winds that surround the planet in belts push ocean currents so that those currents move in regular and predictable patterns. Oceanic and atmospheric currents work together to transfer heat from tropical regions to temperate and polar regions, moderating global temperatures. The oceans provide resources, such as fossil fuels and pharmaceuticals, and they are full of the promise of other resources, such as alternative energy sources and mineral wealth. The oceans are the most biologically productive places on the Earth; ocean plants create more food energy than plants anywhere else. This food energy is the foundation for amazing ecosystems that harbor an incredible diversity of plants and animals. These rich biological resources provide a vital protein source for a substantial number of humans. Without the oceans, Earth's people would be hungrier.

Besides furnishing resources, the oceans provide a sink for wastes. People have long thought that the vastness of the oceans would hide, dilute, or dissipate their solid and liquid rubbish, and for much of human history the oceans have provided that service. But now the human population and the quantity of waste it creates have grown so much that the oceans are reaching their limit of what they can absorb. A large amount of the material that pollutes the oceans is dumped intentionally. Both developing and developed nations transport their sewage, often untreated, into the sea in large pipes, while ships empty their bilges at sea. Wastes are also released into the marine environment unintentionally; catastrophic oil spills, like that of the *Exxon Valdez* in Alaska, are deadly examples. Some human activities that seem to be harmless, such as the entry of plant nutrients from detergents and fertilizers into the sea, actually change the makeup of marine life, allowing some organisms to grow at the expense of others and creating zones where virtually nothing can live. Moving species of plants or animals from where they belong to new environments, usually done unintentionally, can also wreak havoc on the native organisms.

Overexploitation threatens many marine species. Fisheries that were once brimming with animals have collapsed or are in danger of collapsing. Some species of marine mammals have been hunted to extinction or nearly so. When hunting decreases, some species recover, but some do not, and no one is sure why. Fish farming holds the promise of supplying people with much needed protein, but such farming has costs that include damage to the environment and to native species.

In many countries, coastal communities thrive economically, drawing in residents and tourists. Coastal environments are sometimes harmed by the development that people bring. Hotels, businesses, and parking lots obliterate the habitats that were once home to native animals and plants. Tourists damage coastal regions as they dive and swim in the water, lie on the beach, buy souvenirs, and encourage the building of resorts and theme parks. Human activities change the makeup of gases in the atmosphere, create an ozone hole, and stimulate global warming, all of which have their effects on the sea. Coral reefs, in particular, are harmed by rising ocean temperatures.

Part One of this volume describes the geology, chemistry, physics, and biology of the ocean and ocean basins. Scientists approach the study of the oceans by applying the knowledge and techniques from each of these disciplines to their understanding of the sea. The rest of the volume focuses on the commodities that the oceans provide to people and the impacts people have on the oceans. Part Two discusses resources found in seawater and in the seabed: minerals, energy, food, and routes for transportation, among others. Part Three describes the oceans as a dump for pollutants, and the effects of pollution on the seas and their life. Part Three also includes a chapter on the effects of ozone loss and global warming on the oceans. In Part Four, human impacts on marine animals and their habitats are described; these include overfishing, excess hunting, fish farming, and habitat destruction. Part Five discusses what governments should do to protect the oceans and describes what individuals can do to make a difference.

THE OCEANS

The Ocean Basins
and the Coasts

The chapters of Part One look at the major sub-disciplines of oceanography: geological, chemical, physical, and biological. This chapter briefly presents the topics of geological oceanography, why there are continents and oceans, how ocean basins form, and how continents move around on the solid Earth. The features of the different types of coastlines, the processes that form them, and the extraordinary geologic features of the seafloor are also described.

THE WORLD OCEAN

Oceans cover 71% of the Earth's surface, but they are not evenly distributed. The Southern Hemisphere is 75% ocean and only 25% land, but the Northern Hemisphere is nearly evenly divided between land and ocean.

People think of the oceans as being distinct, since they are separated by the landmasses and have their own characteristics. But all of the oceans are interconnected. In fact, a water molecule could circulate to

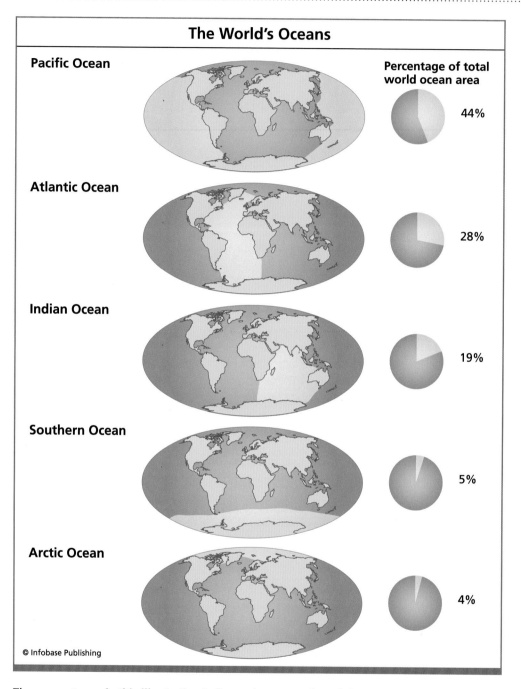

The percentages in this illustration indicate the proportion of the total world ocean area made up by each named ocean (excludes adjacent seas).

every portion of each ocean if given enough time. The circular Pacific Ocean covers more than one-third of the Earth's surface. Although its name means "peaceful," it is home to many of the world's largest storms and to much of its earthquake and volcanic activity. The small, triangular Indian Ocean lies mostly in the Southern Hemisphere. The S-shaped Atlantic covers more than one-fifth of the Earth's surface. At its northern reaches lies the relatively small and landlocked Arctic Ocean, which is nearly cut off from the Atlantic by underwater barriers. The Southern Ocean, first recognized in 2000, incorporates water from the southern reaches of the three largest oceans and is defined by the swift Antarctic Circumpolar Current that circles Antarctica. And there are also **seas**, which are defined as landlocked or partially landlocked bodies of water, such as the Mediterranean Sea.

The oceans are the largest reservoir in the Earth's **hydrologic cycle**. In this cycle, water evaporates from the sea surface to enter the atmosphere as **water vapor** (water in its gaseous state). Then, when conditions are right, water vapor condenses into liquid droplets that form clouds. The droplets may join together to precipitate as rain, snow, hail, or sleet. On land, the water may become frozen into a glacier; may travel through lakes, streams, and ponds; or may become groundwater (water that infiltrates the ground to reside in an underground rock layer). The water flows downstream and, ultimately, into the ocean. All seawater and a small amount of lake water is **saline** (salty).

WHY THE EARTH HAS OCEAN BASINS

The simple answer to the question of why the Earth has oceans is that it has deep basins and water to fill them with. The more complex answer involves how these basins form and how they differ from the continents.

The Earth's **crust** is its rocky outermost layer. There are two types of crust: **Oceanic crust** is thin and relatively dense (**density** is the mass per unit volume of a substance). Oceanic crust is made of **basalt**, a dark-colored rock that flows from volcanoes. **Continental**

crust is thick, relatively low density, and made of many different types of rocks. The differences in crust types explain why there are ocean basins.

Beneath the Earth's crust is its **mantle**. Although the mantle is solid rock, some of it is so hot that it can flow like toothpaste. Both oceanic and continental crust "float" on the mantle the way a boat floats on water, but dense oceanic crust sinks deeper into the mantle as if the boat were carrying weighty cargo. The less dense and thicker continental crust floats higher and therefore is elevated. Oceanic crust provides a basin that, when filled with water, becomes an ocean.

Continental and oceanic crusts are different because they form differently. Continental crust is produced by a multitude of Earth processes (volcanic eruptions, unification of rock fragments, among many others) that act over timescales of up to billions of years. New ocean crust is continually being created as basalt lava rises up from the mantle and erupts along lines of deep-sea volcanism known as **mid-ocean ridges** that run through the ocean basins. The eruption of new basalt pushes the older crust out laterally away from the ridge. For this reason, oceanic crust is youngest at the ridge and gets older as it moves farther from the ridge crest.

Old oceanic crust is destroyed at arc-shaped depressions in the seafloor known as deep-sea **trenches**. When the crust reaches a trench, it plunges in and reenters the mantle, a process called **subduction**. The subduction of oceanic crust into the mantle is not smooth, and subduction zones are associated with violent earthquakes and volcanic eruptions. The Pacific basin experiences violent geological activity because it is lined with subduction zones.

The spreading of oceanic crust outward in both directions from mid-ocean ridges, called **seafloor spreading**, pushes continents around the planet's surface. The creation and destruction of oceanic crust and the movements of slabs of oceanic and continental crust are part of the theory of **plate tectonics**. (A **theory** is an explanation for a natural phenomenon that is supported by many observations, seems to have no major inconsistencies, and is accepted by nearly all practitioners in the discipline.)

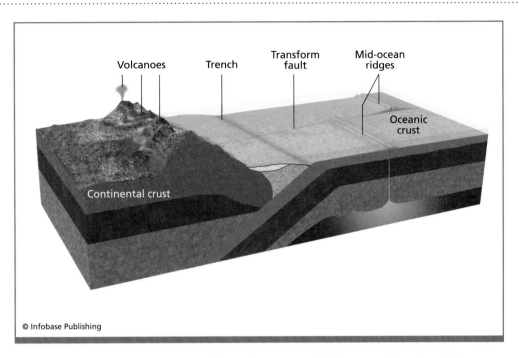

Volcanoes   Trench   Transform fault   Mid-ocean ridges

Oceanic crust

Continental crust

© Infobase Publishing

When older oceanic crust meets continental crust or still older ocean floor, it will plunge into a subduction zone beneath that crust, creating volcanoes.

COASTS: THE TRANSITION FROM CONTINENT TO OCEAN

Land meets sea in the region known as the **coast**. There are two main types of coasts, each characterized by its own distinctive features. Geologically active areas, where there are periodic earthquakes and volcanic eruptions such as near a subduction zone, have rocky shorelines with little sand. The Oregon coast—known for its small sandy beaches separated by steep cliffs—is located inland from a subduction zone.

Geologically passive areas, like the eastern United States, are typified by long sandy beaches. The beaches are made of **sediments**—pieces of rocks and minerals that are shaped by waves, currents, and tides. Sands are common beach sediments. **Longshore currents** move sediments parallel to the beach. Longshore currents may deposit sediments that waves shape into islands that lie parallel to the mainland and are separated from it by a narrow water body known as a **lagoon**.

These **barrier islands** rim the Atlantic seaboard and the Gulf Coast of the United States. Examples include Galveston Island, Texas; Atlantic City, New Jersey; and Miami Beach, Florida. Most of these islands have become heavily developed. Where a river drops sediments at the seashore, **deltas**—such as the Mississippi delta—take shape. On either type of coast, those in geologically active or geologically passive areas, there may be river-carved valleys that were flooded by rising sea level, such as Chesapeake Bay, located on the East Coast of the United States, and Monterey Bay, located on the West Coast.

Moving seaward from the coast, the transition from continent to ocean is known as the **continental margin**, which is the submerged edge of the continents. The shoreline can be anywhere along the continental margin, depending on the sea level. The nearest portion of the continental margin to the shore is called the **continental shelf**, the sediment-covered drowned edge of a continent.

FEATURES OF THE OCEAN BASINS

Until recent decades, scientists thought that the ocean floor was entirely flat. Yet astonishingly, seawater conceals the Earth's longest mountain range, deepest trenches, steepest canyons, and flattest plains.

The mid-ocean ridge system is an enormous range of interconnected volcanic mountains that extends over 36,000 miles (60,000 kilometers), and takes up one-third of the ocean floor. The ridge rises as much as 1.25 miles (2 km) above the seafloor and emerges in spots to become oceanic islands such as Iceland, Easter Island, and the Galapagos Islands.

Near the edges of the ocean basins are the arc-shaped trenches where subduction occurs. These trenches are located primarily in the Pacific Ocean and are the deepest places on Earth. Trenches plunge to about 1.9 to 3.7 miles (3 to 6 kilometers) into the seafloor. The deepest trench, the Mariana in the western Pacific, is 36,163 feet (11,022 meters) below sea level, deeper than Mt. Everest is high.

Mid-ocean ridges are home to **hydrothermal** (hot water) **vents**, deep-sea hot springs that erupt where seawater contacts hot lava from beneath the earth or newly formed ocean crust. Vent fluids as hot as 660°F (350°C) shoot out into the cold ocean, creating billowing streams of metal sulfide minerals, called **black smokers**. Vent fluids are dominated by **methane** (natural gas) and hydrogen. The minerals fall near the vent, creating towering metal-sulfide "chimneys." When the vents were discovered in 1977, scientists were shocked to find that they were home to a thriving community of sea animals. "Discovery of the hydrothermal vent communities is one of the most exciting developments in oceanography in the past 50 years," said Jim Yoder, director of the National Science Foundation's Division of Ocean Sciences, in a 2002 press release from the Woods Hole Oceanographic Institution.

Black smokers at a hydrothermal vent site in the Pacific Ocean. *(© Science VU/WHOI/Visuals Unlimited)*

Seamounts are individual volcanoes—extinct or active—that rise high above the sea floor (but not above sea level, where they would be considered islands). Only a small part of the seafloor is as flat and featureless as the entire seafloor was once thought to be. The **abyssal plains** are areas of seafloor that have been made flat by being buried beneath multiple layers of sediment.

OCEAN BASIN SEDIMENTS

Sediments from both land and marine sources coat the features of the ocean basins. Most seafloor sediments are brought in from the continents and are concentrated near the continental margins.

Deep-sea sediments are tiny particles of dust, rock, or the shells of living organisms that fall through the water depths and accumulate on the ocean floor. **Plankton**, which consist of tiny marine plants (**phytoplankton**) and animals (**zooplankton**), inhabit much of the ocean surface. When plankton die, their shells fall to the bottom of the sea to form sediments of calcareous ($CaCO_3$) or siliceous (SiO_2) material, depending on the shell composition. These biological sediments are more prevalent below locations where life is abundant. Sometimes these sediments are buried deeply enough to form **fossil fuels**, organic compounds composed of hydrogen and carbon that are a major energy source for modern society. Hydrogenous sediments are

How Scientists Learn About the Sea

To learn more about the ocean than is possible from standing on the shore or peering over the deck of a ship, oceanographers need specially designed tools. Research ships travel out to sea for periods ranging from days to months. These ships carry equipment that can be used to sample sediment, rocks, water, and marine life, and that even can be used to make maps. A **gravity corer** is a hollow tube deployed on a cable that accelerates down into the deep. When the tube reaches the ocean bottom, it slices into the sediment and collects a nicely layered sample inside. Seafloor rocks are collected with a **dredge**, a giant rectangular bucket that is dragged behind the ship. To collect seawater samples, bottles are placed at regular intervals along a cable and lowered to the correct depth. A weight dropped along the cable closes each bottle, trapping the water inside.

A **bathymetric map** shows the three-dimensional geographic features of the seafloor on a two-dimensional map. A device towed behind a ship sends out sound waves that strike the ocean bottom and then echo back to the ship. The amount of time it takes for a sound wave to make a round trip allows scientists to calculate the distance from the seafloor to the device. As this information is compiled, a map of the seafloor emerges.

Submersibles are small diving craft that can move underwater independently of the mother ship. The battery-operated submersible *Alvin*, for example, can descend to more than 13,000 feet (4,000 m) carrying a pilot and two passengers who collect samples, take photos and video, and make rocky or metallic materials that precipitate out of the water. **Manganese nodules**, baseball-sized rocks of metal oxides, grow around a "core," such as a rock, grain of sand, or shark's tooth. The accumulation rate of metal is exceedingly slow, about 0.04 inches (1 millimeter) per one million years.

Marine sediments can be used by scientists to understand the geologic history of the ocean region in which the sediments lie. If they are undisturbed, marine sediments can be read like a book, with the earliest chapter at the bottom and the most recent chapter on top. In fact, much of what scientists know about plate tectonics, the history of the ocean, the evolution of marine life, ancient current patterns,

accurate descriptions of what they see. Submersibles offer scientists their best view of the deep ocean, but visiting the deep sea can be dangerous. Submersibles need strong housing to keep from collapsing under the enormous pressure, life support for their occupants, and elaborate safety protocols.

Because **remotely operated vehicles (ROVs)** carry no human passengers, they can visit even more dangerous locations. The ROV *Jason* photographed rooms inside the *Titanic*, and the ROV *Argo* has traveled dangerously close to hydrothermal vents. ROVs are attached to the mother ship by a fiber-optic cable that returns data and video in real time. Scientists on board the mother ship can interpret data and make decisions about what to explore while the vehicle is at its target.

Drilling is the best way to collect rocks and sediment from the seafloor. The Integrated Ocean Drilling Program (IODP), an international consortium of marine research institutions, operates the drilling ship *Joides Resolution*. The ship's drill cuts through the layers of sediments and rocks and returns them to the ship via the drill pipe. This maintains the integrity of the sediment and rock layers better than any other technique.

Satellites collect information on water movements from buoys, unmanned platforms, or ships at sea. Onboard instruments detect temperatures, concentrations of plankton, and many other features of the sea surface. Satellite data can be integrated with shipboard data to give a detailed view of what is happening in the ocean.

and the Earth's climate has been told by sediments from the bottom of the sea.

WRAP-UP

The Earth has oceans because oceanic crust is thinner and denser than continental crust. Oceanic crust forms as lava erupts at mid-ocean ridges. The creation of new seafloor pushes continents around the Earth's surface. Old oceanic crust plunges into deep-sea trenches and reenters the mantle. The processes that create the seafloor and move the continents are known as plate tectonics. These processes are responsible for nearly all geologic activity, such as volcanic eruptions and earthquakes. Mid-ocean ridges and trenches are two of the varied features found on the seafloor. Some of the features of coastal regions are dependent on nearness to a subduction zone. Sediments from the ocean floor tell geologists the history of a region, whether it is near shore, beneath an active life zone, or is favorable for the precipitation of metallic materials.

Seawater

Without water, the ocean basins would sit empty. Fortunately, planet Earth has lots of water to fill them. This chapter describes some of the features of that water—the topics of chemical oceanography—such as the structure and properties of water molecules, the types of salts found in seawater, the acidity of the seas, and other chemical properties of the oceans.

THE WATER MOLECULE

Water has many unique properties that are the result of the structure of the water **molecule**. A molecule is the smallest unit of a substance that has all the properties of that substance. Water, with the chemical formula H_2O, is made of **atoms** of hydrogen and oxygen. An atom is the smallest unit of a chemical element having the properties of that element. At its center is a **nucleus**, which contains **protons** with small positive electrical charges and **neutrons**, which have no charge. **Electrons** orbit the nucleus in shells; each electron has a small negative electrical charge. If the number of protons and electrons in an atom are equal, the atom has no charge.

Atoms are most stable when their outer electron shells are full, and an atom will give, take, or share one or more electrons to achieve this stability. An **ion** is an atom that has gained or lost an electron. If an atom loses an electron, it has lost a negative charge, so it becomes a positive ion. If an atom gains an electron, it gains a negative charge and becomes a negative ion. A molecule is made of more than one atom or ion and has no electrical charge.

Hydrogen is the smallest and simplest atom; it is one proton orbited by one electron. Oxygen has eight protons and eight orbiting electrons, two in its inner electron shell and six in its outer electron shell. Since oxygen has six electrons and needs eight to have a full outer shell, and hydrogen has one electron and needs two or zero to have a full (or empty) outer shell, in a water molecule each hydrogen atom shares its single electron with the oxygen to make **covalent bonds**. With covalent bonds, an atom retains its own electrons but shares one or more of them with another atom, so each atom has a full outer electron shell.

Water is a **polar molecule**; the positive and negative charges within it are not evenly distributed, so one side is positive and one side is negative. With polar molecules, the positive side of one water molecule is attracted to the negative side of another. This forms a **hydrogen bond**, which binds the molecules loosely together. Hydrogen bonds are relatively weak compared to covalent bonds. Hydrogen bonds are responsible for water's **surface tension**, the feature that causes water to form a drop (because the molecules are attracted to each other) rather than spreading out in a film. Despite their weakness, the hydrogen bonds between water molecules take energy to break—energy that is absorbed by the water.

ADDING SALT TO WATER

The water molecule's polarity makes water a great **solvent**. More substances—solids, liquids, or gases—dissolve in water than in any other common liquid. Water's ability as a solvent explains why so

Water as a Solvent

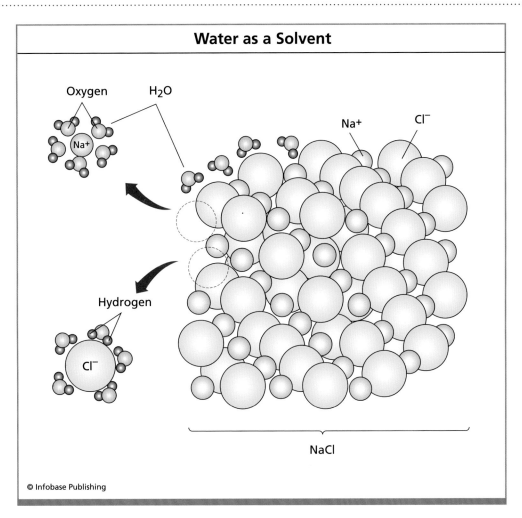

© Infobase Publishing

Water can dissolve a greater range of substances, and in greater amounts, than any other common liquid. Salt dissolves readily in water because positively charged sodium ions (Na^+) tend to be pulled into solution by the slightly negatively charged oxygen atoms of water molecules. Negatively charged chloride ions (Cl^-) are pulled into solution by the slightly positively charged hydrogen atoms in water.

much of it is saline. Sodium chloride (NaCl), also called table salt, is the most prevalent type of salt found in water.

In a solid NaCl crystal, the sodium (Na) ion has one electron orbiting in its outer shell; chlorine (Cl) needs one electron to have a full outer shell. Na gives its extra electron to Cl, creating NaCl. A bond in which one atom gives its electron to another atom is called an **ionic bond**. When a salt crystal immersed in water dissolves, the positively charged Na ion is pulled off by the negative side of a water molecule, and the negatively charged Cl ion is pulled off by the positive side of a water molecule. Water molecules surround the Na and Cl ions, and in time the salt crystal dissolves. The ions are reunited only if enough water evaporates so that they are no longer surrounded by it.

On average, seawater is 96.5% (*percent* can be thought of as parts per hundred) water and 3.5% dissolved substances, most of which are salts. Salinity is usually expressed as parts per thousand (ppt). Average seawater is 35 ppt salt, and ocean salinity varies between 33 and 37 ppt. More than 86% of the dissolved substances in seawater are Na and Cl, with other mineral salts—sulfate, magnesium, calcium, potassium, and bicarbonate—bringing the total to 99%. Many minor components make up the remaining 1% of the substances in seawater. Minor elements are found in concentrations greater than one part per million (ppm); trace elements are found in amounts less than 1 ppm and so are often expressed in parts per billion (ppb).

Although they are present in tiny quantities, some trace elements are essential to marine life. Biologically important ions are known as **nutrients**. These chemicals include elements that are critical for cell growth (nitrogen and phosphorus) and for building shells and skeletons (silicon and calcium).

Most of the gases that are found in the atmosphere dissolve in water at the ocean's surface. Because each of the gases has a different **solubility**, or ability to dissolve, in seawater, they are not present in the same amounts as they are in the atmosphere. The three major gases that make up 99% of the gases in the ocean are shown in the table on page 17.

Just as atmospheric gases are essential for land organisms, dissolved gases in seawater are crucial for marine organisms. Marine plants use carbon dioxide (CO_2) for **photosynthesis**. In this process, plants take CO_2 and water (H_2O) to create sugar (food energy) and oxygen (O_2) in the presence of sunlight. Many marine animals

Major Gases in the Atmosphere and Ocean

GAS	PERCENT IN ATMOSPHERE, BY VOLUME	PERCENT IN SEAWATER, BY VOLUME	CONCEN-TRATION IN SEAWATER, IN PPM BY MASS
Nitrogen (N_2)	78.08	48	10–18
Oxygen (O_2)	20.95	36	0–13
Carbon dioxide (CO_2)	0.035	15	64–107

breathe in oxygen through their skin or their gills, in a process called **respiration**. This process uses oxygen to convert sugar into energy that plants and animals can use.

WHY THE SEA IS SALTY

Water enters the oceans directly from rain or by inflow from streams or groundwater. Although none of these sources seem salty, seawater itself is salty. So where does the salt in seawater come from?

As water molecules move across the land or infiltrate into the ground, their polarity attracts ions from broken-down rocks. Many ions—sodium, calcium, magnesium, and bicarbonate, among others— are present in fresh water in tiny amounts. Other ions—chlorine, carbon dioxide, sulfur, hydrogen, fluorine, and nitrogen—have sources in the deep sea. The ions are released when seawater percolates through new oceanic crust, or they are discharged from hydrothermal vents.

Salts are continually being added to the ocean, yet the sea does not get saltier because the amount of salt added to the sea equals the amount being taken out. Salts leave the ocean when seawater in shallow regions evaporates, which leaves salts behind. Salts are blown onto land by the wind; are used by organisms to create shells, which ultimately become buried in seafloor sediments; or they are extracted from circulating seawater by hot basalt rocks. Some ions attach onto clays and are removed from the water when the clay falls as sediment.

ACIDS IN SEAWATER

Acidity is another important feature of the chemistry of seawater. When H_2O breaks apart, it forms hydrogen ions (H^+) and hydroxyl ions (OH^-). In pure water, the amount of H^+ equals the amount of OH^-. If a substance that is added to water brings about an excess of H^+, the solution becomes an **acid**. If OH^- is in excess, the solution is **alkaline**.

Acidity and alkalinity are measured on the **pH** scale, with numbers from 0 to 14. The H in pH refers to the quantity of free positively charged hydrogen ions. Pure water is neutral, with a pH of 7. Numbers higher than 7 are alkaline (also called basic); numbers lower than 7 are acidic. The lowest numbers are the strongest acids and highest numbers are the strongest bases. The pH scale is logarithmic, so a change in one unit reflects a tenfold change in acidity.

Average seawater is slightly alkaline, with a pH of about 8.0. Adding CO_2 adds carbonic acid, which lowers pH. In deep waters, below approximately 2.5 to 3 miles (4 to 4.8 km), pH is around 7.5 since CO_2 is added to the water by respiration of animals and the decay of organic material. This water is acidic enough to dissolve **calcium carbonate ($CaCO_3$)** sediments. For this reason, these sediments cannot exist in the deep ocean. Near the surface, the pH is about 8.5 because these waters are warm and can hold less dissolved CO_2. Photosynthesis in surface waters also depletes CO_2.

Seawater acidity does not change much because the ocean system has an acid-base **buffer**. If acid is added to seawater, the excess H^+ combines with bicarbonate ion (HCO_3^-) to form carbonic acid (H_2CO_3). This dissociates into CO_2 and H_2O. If an alkaline solution

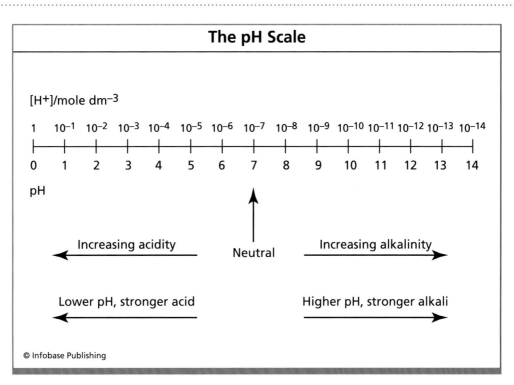

The pH Scale

[H+]/mole dm^{-3}

1   10^{-1} 10^{-2} 10^{-3} 10^{-4} 10^{-5} 10^{-6} 10^{-7} 10^{-8} 10^{-9} 10^{-10} 10^{-11} 10^{-12} 10^{-13} 10^{-14}

0   1   2   3   4   5   6   7   8   9   10   11   12   13   14

pH

Increasing acidity   Neutral   Increasing alkalinity

Lower pH, stronger acid   Higher pH, stronger alkali

© Infobase Publishing

A neutral solution has a pH of 7.0; less than 7.0 is acidic and greater than 7.0 is alkaline. Hydrogen ion concentration is shown on the upper axis of the scale.

is added, the HCO_3^- goes to carbonate (CO_3^{2-}) and H^+, causing the solution to become more acidic. The addition of CO_2 to surface waters, due to volcanic eruptions or fossil-fuel emissions, forms carbonic acid (H_2CO_3), which dissociates into HCO_3^- and H^+.

WRAP-UP

Seawater is composed predominantly of water, which is a polar molecule. The molecule's polarity is why seawater is salty; fresh water traveling across or infiltrating into the land surface picks up salt ions and brings them into the ocean. Ocean salinity does not increase over time because other processes remove excess salts. Besides salts, seawater contains nutrients, gases, organic compounds, and other minor components that are essential for supporting marine life. Seawater is slightly alkaline and its acidity does not change much because it is buffered for acids and bases. At depths where the seawater is more acidic, such as in the deep sea, carbonate sediments dissolve.

Water Movement

Seawater is not stagnant but is constantly in motion. The motions of ocean water described in this chapter are in the realm of physical oceanography. The global wind belts push the water along in currents that travel around the sea surface. Where seawater becomes dense enough, it descends into, and flows through, the deep sea. Ocean currents carry heat from warm regions to cooler regions and vice versa, moderating temperatures around the planet. Winds, particularly from storms, create waves at the sea surface. Tides are the result of the gravitational attraction of the Moon and Sun.

SURFACE OCEAN CURRENTS

Surface ocean currents circulate in a predictable pattern no matter what is happening with the wind and weather. The water is pushed in the directions of the following major wind belts: the trade winds, from east to west between the equator and 30°N or 30°S; the westerlies, from west to east in the mid-latitudes; and the polar easterlies, from east to

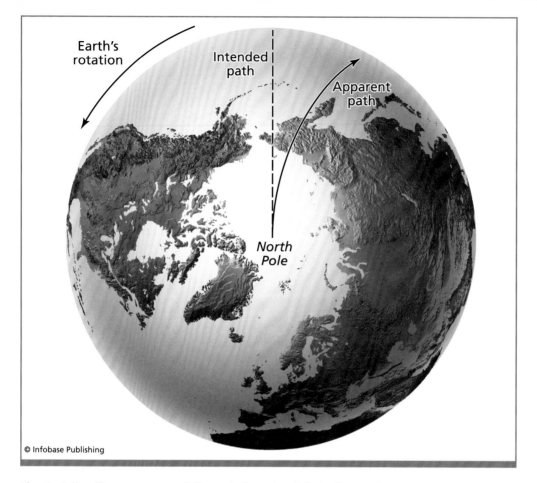

The Coriolis effect appears to deflect winds to the right in the Northern Hemisphere and to the left in the Southern Hemisphere.

west between 50° and 60°N or S and the poles. Surface currents travel with the wind until they run into a continent and are forced to turn. Due to the Coriolis Effect, the surface currents turn to the right in the Northern Hemisphere and to the left in the Southern Hemisphere. (The **Coriolis effect** is the tendency for any freely moving body to appear to shift sideways from its course because the Earth's surface is rotating beneath it.) After traveling parallel to the continent's shores, the water joins an east-to-west or west-to-east moving current that is flowing back in the direction from where it first came. When it

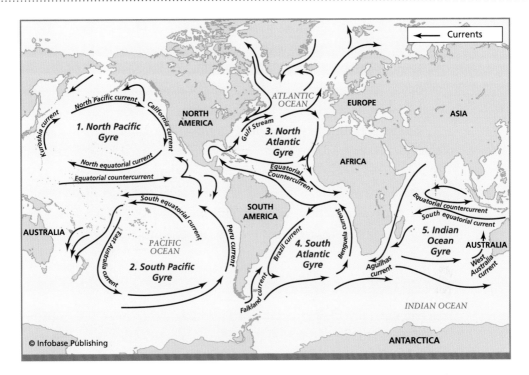

The major surface ocean currents. The five gyres are the North and South Pacific, the North and South Atlantic, and the Indian.

reaches the continent on the other side of the ocean, it turns right or left depending on the hemisphere in which it is located.

The result is a circular current called a **gyre**, which rotates clockwise in the Northern Hemisphere and counterclockwise in the Southern Hemisphere. The five major ocean gyres are centered in the North and South Pacific, the North and South Atlantic, and the Indian Ocean. Only one current—the Antarctic Circumpolar Current, also called the West Wind Drift—travels freely around the globe.

Due to friction, surface ocean currents move much more slowly than the wind that drags them. Currents on the western sides of gyres (off the east coast of continents) are swifter, narrower, and deeper than currents on the eastern sides. These **western boundary currents** carry warm water from the equator toward the poles. The largest of them is the Gulf Stream, which travels up eastern North America and averages 43 miles (70 km) wide and 1,500 feet (450 m) deep. At its swiftest, the Gulf Stream moves at about 100 miles (160 km) a day. Western boundary currents are more intense because water piles up at the eastern edges of continents, due to the rotation of the Earth and to the piling up of water by the trade winds.

Eastern boundary currents on the eastern sides of gyres bring cooler water toward the equator. These oceanic rivers are shallower, broader, and slower than western boundary currents. The centers of the gyres have little horizontal or vertical circulation because the water there is generally warmer, and therefore less dense, than the water beneath it. Therefore, it remains at the surface.

DEEP OCEAN CURRENTS

Ocean water also flows from the surface to the deep ocean and from the deep ocean to the surface. Vertical movements are due to the density differences of seawater, which are a function of temperature and salinity. Cold water is denser than warm water, and saline water is denser than fresh water. Denser water sinks beneath less dense water.

Changes in the temperature and salinity of a water mass take place at the sea surface. The water may be cooled by polar air or warmed by the Sun. In the polar regions, frigid air cools water at the sea surface, and sea-ice formation increases the water's salinity, making it very dense. When the surface water becomes as dense as the water beneath it, it sinks. This is called **downwelling**. As this surface water sinks, it pushes the deep water along the seafloor to generate a deep sea current. Dense water created in the North Atlantic and near Antarctica pushes water around the sea bottom to drive global ocean circulation. This process brings gases and nutrients, which are used by mid-level and bottom-dwelling organisms, from the surface into the deep sea.

Deep water mixes with less dense water as it flows, causing its density to decrease. The water rises to the surface at **upwelling** zones, which are found along coastlines or in long equatorial currents where surface water is deflected by the Coriolis effect, and deep water rises

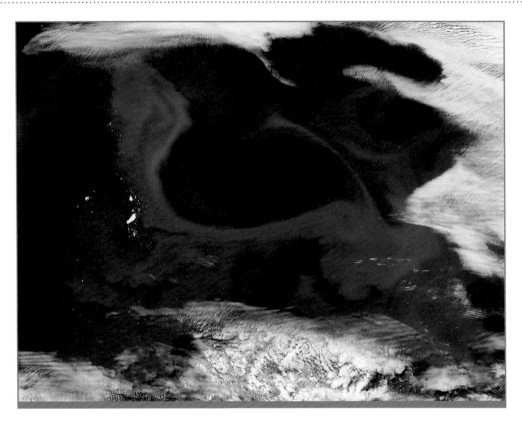

A phytoplankton bloom appears as large blue and green swirls in this photograph of the waters near South Georgia, a remote island in the south Atlantic Ocean.

up to fill the void. Upwelling water is nutrient-rich because it comes from the deep where, over many decades or centuries, the remains of dead plants and animals falling from the surface have accumulated and where there are few organisms to make use of them. When the nutrient-rich upwelling water is hit by sunlight at the surface, phytoplankton bloom and animals thrive. During a plankton bloom, plankton numbers may increase so dramatically that the water turns yellow, brown, or green.

Upwelling water works its way back into the North Atlantic by way of a variety of surface currents. Once there, it sinks and begin its journey around the globe again. The global ocean current system is

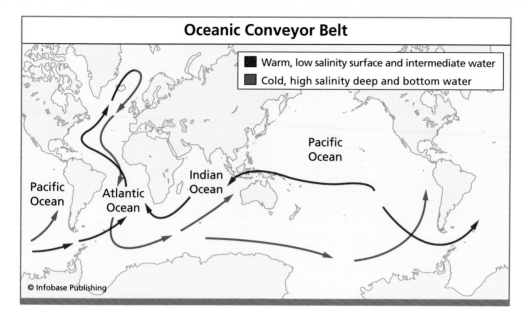

Oceanic Conveyor Belt

■ Warm, low salinity surface and intermediate water
■ Cold, high salinity deep and bottom water

Pacific Ocean

Indian Ocean

Pacific Ocean

Atlantic Ocean

© Infobase Publishing

Global ocean circulation with major surface water movements shown in red and deep water currents shown in blue.

known as the great ocean conveyor. A single water molecule will make the complete circuit around the ocean in about 1,600 years.

WAVES

Local winds, such as those generated by storms, create waves. Once formed, waves travel far from their place of origin, even without wind to push them. In the open ocean, waves travel as rounded swells at 20 to 50 miles per hour (30 to 85 kph). Waves break when they become too tall to be supported by their base. Waves break at sea during rough weather, but most waves do not break until they reach the shore.

When storm winds blow water onto a shoreline, sea level rises in that spot to create **storm surge**. This can raise sea level 25 feet (7.5 m) or more if the water is in a confined bay. Storm surge greatly compounds the damage done by a storm's high winds and rains, especially at high tide. The storm surge that accompanied a tropical storm in November 1970 killed more than 300,000 people in low-lying Bangladesh.

The most deadly waves are not created by wind, but by shocks to ocean water, often in the form of an earthquake. These waves are known as **tsunamis**.

TIDES

Some ocean motions are not caused by weather or earthquakes. Each day, sea level rises and falls due to **tides**, which are produced by the gravitational attraction of the Moon and Sun to the Earth. The Moon has twice the effect on Earth's tides as the Sun because, although the Moon is much smaller than the Sun, it is also closer to the Earth and exerts a much stronger gravitational attraction.

Most places experience two high and two low tides a day. The Moon's gravity tugs on whatever portion of the Earth is directly beneath it; if that portion is water, it creates a bulge known as a high tide. Another high tide forms at the same time on the other side of the planet. However, this high tide is not caused directly by the Moon but by inertial forces, which are the forces that keep a moving object moving. As a result, many ocean locations experience two high tides per day—one as the spot passes beneath the Moon and the other when that same spot is directly on the other side of the Earth, opposite from the Moon.

The tide also rises directly beneath and on the side of the Earth directly opposite the Sun. The highest high tides of the month occur when the Sun's and Moon's tidal bulges are brought together. These occur when the Sun is aligned with the Moon (a new Moon) or is directly opposite the Moon (a full Moon). Because the highest high tides take up so much of the ocean's water, the lowest low tides take place simultaneously at the midway points between the high tides.

A day with the highest high tides and lowest low tides of the month is said to be experiencing spring tides. These days occur every two weeks—during the full Moon, when the Moon is on the opposite side of the Earth from the Sun; and during the new Moon, when the Sun and the Moon are on the same side of the Earth. When the Sun and Moon are at right angles to each other, during neap tides, the difference between high and low tides is at its smallest. Neap tides also occur every two weeks, during the first quarter and third quarter Moon. Because the Moon takes 24 hours and 50 minutes to rotate

Tsunami

Before December 26, 2004, tsunamis were often incorrectly called tidal waves, although they have nothing to do with tides. But when the Boxing Day tsunami spread across the Indian Ocean, striking eight countries and killing around 230,000 people, everyone learned the correct name. In just a few minutes, more than 1.2 million people were left homeless, and many more lost their livelihoods. Coastal **ecosystems** were damaged or destroyed and many near-shore animals, such as dolphins, turtles, and sharks, were washed inland. (An ecosystem contains all the organisms that live in an area, plus the total of water, land, and atmosphere needed to sustain them.)

Tsunamis are usually caused by undersea earthquakes. The Boxing Day earthquake struck 60 miles (100 km) off the northwestern shore of Sumatra, where the Indian plate is subducting beneath the Burma plate. The earthquake measured 9.0 on the Richter scale, the largest the planet had seen in 40 years. The extreme movement of oceanic crust rapidly displaced trillions of tons of water and generated the wave.

Tsunamis travel at speeds up to 500 miles per hour (800 km/h) along the sea surface. The waves are barely noticeable in open water, but they build in height as they approach the shoreline. Within one hour, the wave slammed into Sumatra, and within two hours it reached India. The tsunami reached Africa, its final stop, about eight hours later. Wave heights were greatest near the earthquake epicenter and decreased with distance, ranging from over 33 feet (10 m) at Sumatra down to 13 feet (4 m) at Sri Lanka, Thailand, and Somalia.

Officials did not expect such a massive tsunami to strike from the Indian Ocean, although a few scientists had warned of that possibility. Since the Pacific Rim is lined with subduction zones, most people had thought a devastating tsunami would strike there. Because of this, residents in countries along the Pacific Ocean have had an international tsunami-warning network around the Earth, in locations where there are two high tides a day, high tides are 12 hours and 25 minutes apart. The time lag between a high and a low tide is 6 hours and 12.5 minutes. Although the norm is for two high and two low tides per day, some areas have one high and one low per day.

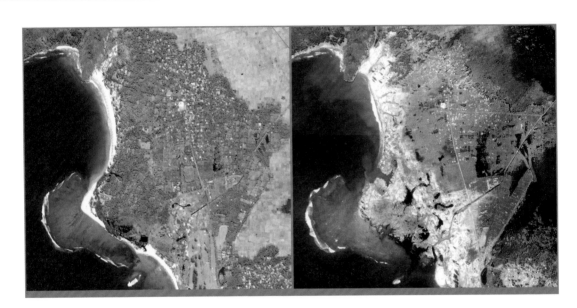

The town of Lhoknga in the Indonesian province of Aceh before (January 10, 2003) and after (December 29, 2004) the Boxing Day tsunami of 2004. Trees, vegetation, and buildings were almost completely destroyed, except for a mosque, the white circular building in the center. When the wave hit shore, its height is thought to have exceeded 50 feet (15 m). *(Images acquired and processed by CRISP, National University of Singapore, IKONOS image © CRISP 2004)*

in operation since 1948; perhaps surprisingly, the system has never been needed. However, even with a good warning system, the regions closest to the earthquake would not be evacuated in time due to the high speed of the waves.

THE OCEANS, WEATHER, AND CLIMATE

The oceans have an enormous influence on the planet's weather and climate. **Hurricanes** grow in summer and autumn when a vast area of the sea surface is 82°F (28°C) or higher, and winds are light. The warm sea surface heats the air above, causing the air to rise. If temperatures within the rising air climb high enough, the air begins to rotate (counterclockwise in the Northern Hemisphere; clockwise in the Southern Hemisphere due to the Coriolis effect). The storm mushrooms upward as hot, spiraling columns of warm air feed on the heat energy from the tropical waters.

Hurricanes are roughly 350 miles (600 km) in diameter and 50,000 feet (15 km) high. When hurricanes reach land, their massive winds push water onto the shore, creating storm surge. Giant waves, up to 50 feet (15 m) high, ride atop the storm surge and cause even greater damage. Where there is little elevation—such as along the Atlantic and Gulf Coasts of the United States, which rise less than 10 feet (3 m) above sea level—flooding may devastate everything in its path. When Hurricane Katrina struck the Gulf of Mexico in August 2005, it took more than 1,300 lives, cost billions of dollars, and brought about the destruction of the uniquely American city of New Orleans, Louisiana, when some of the levees that protected the city from flooding broke.

Ocean currents influence the temperature of the air above them, which can also alter regional climate. As part of the North Atlantic gyre, the Gulf Stream transports warm equatorial waters north along the eastern United States and southeastern Canada, then flows eastward across the North Atlantic. A portion of the current travels north along the coasts of Britain and Norway, bringing equatorial heat to the northern latitudes. The Gulf Stream, therefore, has an enormous effect on the climate of northern Europe. Although London, England, is at 51°N latitude, several degrees north of Quebec in Canada, the climate in London is much more temperate; in London, rain, instead of snow, is the norm in winter.

Like the Gulf Stream, most currents move ceaselessly in the same direction. Sometimes ocean currents change direction, which can

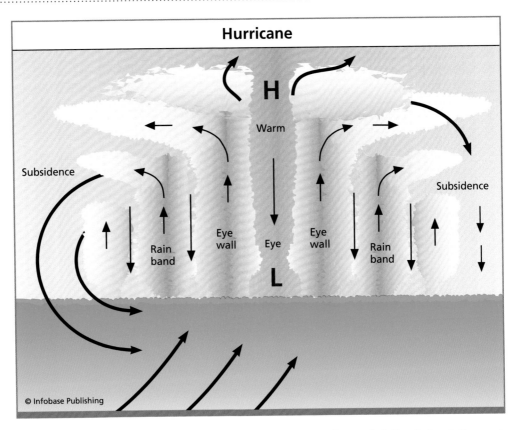

Hurricane

Subsidence

H

Warm

Subsidence

Eye
wall

Eye

Eye
wall

Rain
band

Rain
band

L

© Infobase Publishing

A hurricane is a large, rotating tropical weather system with a well-defined circulation and sustained winds up to 74 mph (119 kph). Hurricanes are products of the warm waters of tropical oceans and warm, moist atmospheres.

bring about acute short-term changes in global weather. The most profound alteration of a current takes place during **El Niño** events.

El Niño

In a normal year, water from the frigid Peru Current travels up South America from the Southern Ocean. The deep water beneath the current is less dense and so it upwells. The upwelled water brings nutrients to the surface, which creates a phytoplankton bloom that supports a thriving ecosystem. The cold current then travels north to the equator, where the relatively cool air above it sinks, creating an atmospheric

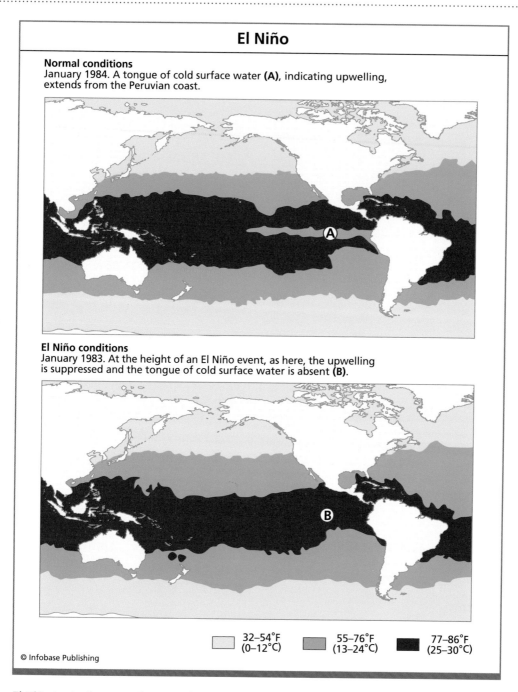

El Niño

Normal conditions
January 1984. A tongue of cold surface water **(A)**, indicating upwelling, extends from the Peruvian coast.

El Niño conditions
January 1983. At the height of an El Niño event, as here, the upwelling is suppressed and the tongue of cold surface water is absent **(B)**.

32–54°F
(0–12°C)   55–76°F
(13–24°C)   77–86°F
(25–30°C)

© Infobase Publishing

El Niño typically occurs in December, when a slackening in trade winds causes the upwelling of cold water off the coast of Peru to slow or stop.

low-pressure zone. At the equator, the current turns west, and the water warms under the equatorial Sun. In the western Pacific, most of the water joins currents moving north and south; some of the water goes back across the equator as a subsurface countercurrent. The rest piles up in the western Pacific, where it becomes hot. The air above the current becomes so hot it rises, forming a low-pressure zone. The trade winds blow across the Pacific from the high-pressure zone in the east to the low-pressure zone in the west.

An El Niño event occurs every three to seven years when too much water piles up in the western Pacific, and both the atmospheric low and high air pressure zones weaken. When this happens, the trade winds reverse direction, dragging warm water rapidly from west to east. When the warm water hits South America, it spreads over the cooler, denser water, shutting off upwelling. The reversal of the trade winds and the replacement of cool, nutrient-rich water with less warm, nutrient-poor water off South America are evidence of an El Niño event. Shutting down upwelling off of South America lessens the phytoplankton bloom, which starves animals higher up the **food chain**. The decline in fish numbers leads to an enormous decrease in sea birds and some marine mammal populations.

The change in wind and ocean circulation also alters weather patterns worldwide. Some regions, such as Ecuador and northern Peru, receive much more rainfall, which transforms their coastal desert into grassland. Other locations, like the western and northeastern United States, are struck by great storms that bring floods and landslides. Flooding also occurs over large parts of South America, Western Europe, and the southern United States. Drought strikes other parts of South America, the western Pacific, southern and northern Africa, southern Asia, and southern Europe.

An El Niño ends after one to two years, when most of the warm western Pacific waters have moved east. When the event is over, normal circulation patterns resume in both the atmosphere and the ocean. Sometimes, during the recovery, the air and water move to the west more vigorously than normal, and unusually cold water accumulates in the eastern Pacific; this situation is called **La Niña**.

WRAP-UP

Ocean water is constantly in motion, in currents, waves, and tides. Currents take a predictable pattern based on the prevailing wind direction. Surface currents transfer heat between regions of different temperature and therefore are responsible for moderating climate. Nearly all waves are created by wind, although earthquakes are responsible for generating deadly waves known as tsunamis. Tides are caused by the gravitational attraction of the Moon and Sun to Earth's water. The time and height of tides varies from day to day during the course of a month. The ocean has an enormous influence on weather, and an El Niño event in the Pacific Ocean can cause extreme weather variations in places halfway around the Earth.

Marine Life

The oceans are perfect environments for a great diversity and abundance of creatures. But life in the sea must survive in very different conditions from life on land: frigid temperatures, high salinity, and little or no light. Despite the differences between terrestrial and marine conditions, the biological principles governing the two major environments are the same. Plants produce food and are eaten by tiny animals, which are eaten by small fish, which are consumed by larger fish and some marine mammals.

WHAT MARINE LIFE NEEDS

All organisms, both marine and terrestrial, must obtain food energy, avoid being eaten, and reproduce, among other activities. The ways that these tasks are accomplished vary greatly within and between the two different environments of land and sea.

Photosynthesis provides usable energy for nearly the entire marine **food web**, which comprises the linked food chains that make up the biological portion of an ecosystem. Plants need the same materials for photosynthesis in the ocean that they need on land: water, light, carbon dioxide, and nutrients. Water, of course, is ubiquitous in the ocean, but light is restricted. Sunlight only penetrates the upper 160 feet (50 m) of the sea, the region known as the **photic zone**. The entire rest of the ocean, called the **aphotic zone**, is dark. Because plants can only live in the photic zone, most marine animals reside there, too. Light in the polar regions is seasonal: no daylight in winter and constant light in summer. As a result, the abundance of life in these areas also follows seasonal patterns.

Marine plants never lack for CO_2 since it is highly soluble in seawater. However, oxygen (O_2), which animals need to burn food for energy, is not soluble. Although O_2 concentrations vary, on average only 1/100 the amount of oxygen in the air is found in the ocean. Environments with no oxygen, including some warm surface waters and some deep isolated basins, are **anaerobic**. Environments with oxygen are **aerobic**.

All organisms need nutrients to make or utilize food or to build hard parts (such as a shell). The essential nutrients in the ocean are nitrates and phosphates, which are needed by the organism's cells, and silica and calcium for making shells and bones. Nutrients come from runoff draining from land, upwelling seawater from the deep, recycling from other organisms, or sediments found on the continental shelf.

The materials marine organisms need for survival are not present in the environment in unlimited quantities. When conditions are right, the number of individuals in a **species** (organisms that can or do interbreed) will increase until something—perhaps iron or oxygen—runs out. This becomes the **limiting factor** for that organism because it restricts the number of individuals of that species that may exist. If the amount of the substance that was limiting increases, for example, when sunlight hits the polar region in the spring, the population of the organism will grow until something else becomes limiting.

ADAPTATIONS TO LIFE IN THE SEA

To survive, a species must be well-adapted to its environment. (An **adaptation** is a structure or behavior that is inheritable, that is, able to be passed on to the next generation by the organism's **genes**.) A well-adapted organism has structures and behaviors that serve it well in its environment. It is more likely to live to adulthood and have many healthy offspring. In this way, the organism passes its genes on to the next generation and gives that generation its best chance of being adapted to its environment. If the environment changes, the species must then evolve by the process of natural selection.

Although ocean conditions are harsh, they are less variable than conditions on land. Ocean temperatures can be extreme but are mostly stable. More than 90% of the ocean is consistently cold, less than 41°F (5°C). Surface temperatures are more variable, between 28°F and 104°F (−2°C and 40°C), but within a single region of the ocean the range is much smaller.

To live in cold water, most marine organisms are **ectotherms**; their body temperatures are the same as the surrounding water. These "cold-blooded" animals are slow moving and slow growing. Ectotherms are adapted to a specific water temperature, and the distribution of many of these species mirrors the pattern of sea-surface temperatures. Ectotherms' rates of biological activity, such as heartbeat, double with every 18°F (10°C) rise in water temperature. Thus, tropical fish grow faster, swim faster, reproduce more frequently, are smaller, and have shorter lives than cold-water fish.

Birds and mammals are **endotherms**. These "warm-blooded" animals keep their body temperatures nearly constant, independent of the temperature of their surroundings. Endotherms fuel their warmth by eating a lot of food, and maintain their body temperature with insulation; for instance, marine birds maintain their body temperature with feathers, while marine mammals maintain theirs with fur and maybe a thick layer of blubber. Marine endotherms have much higher body temperatures than their surroundings; they can tolerate a large range of water temperatures and live in a wide variety of environments.

Evolution by Natural Selection

Evolution by natural selection is responsible for both the incredible diversity and the similarities in life that we see on our planet. **Evolution** means change over time. The theory of evolution describes how creatures come to be successful in the extraordinary number of **habitats** that are available to them—environments that differ from each other in climate, resource availability, and predators, to name just a few. Different habitats include such diverse locations as the Arctic, with frigid temperatures and vast seasonal differences in light; the desert, with its relentless sun and months-long droughts; and the tropics, where the climate is warm and wet and the living conditions are generally favorable. Each habitat is full of organisms that are uniquely adapted for life under those conditions. If the environment changes, the species must evolve. As the revolutionary biologist Charles Darwin said in *The Origin of Species*, "It is not the strongest of the species that survives, nor the most intelligent that survives. It is the one that is the most adaptable to change."

Natural selection is the mechanism for evolution laid out by Darwin, who recognized that the world is a dangerous place and that many young organisms will be eaten by predators or will die in a harsh environment before they reach reproductive age. Because of this, all species produce more offspring than are needed to replace the parents. All young are different from each other, and some are better suited for survival; those are more likely to reproduce and pass their favorable traits on to their offspring. The organisms that are less fit for their environment do not survive to reproduce. Over time, the favorable traits are selected, and the unfavorable traits die out.

Entirely new traits will be introduced into a species' genes by **mutation**. Mutations are random, and most are either neutral or harmful. Occasionally, one helps a species to adapt to its environment. If enough changes take place over time, a new species will arise. Sometimes the new species will come back into contact with the original one. If the new species is better adapted to the environment, it may drive the original species to extinction by producing more offspring that survive to reproduce.

Seawater is more saline than the body fluids of marine organisms. To deal with excess salt, most marine animals have a semi-permeable membrane that keeps their body fluids separate from seawater. To achieve balance, the salts go from regions of high salt concentration to regions of low salt concentration, and water moves from areas of high water concentration (low salinity) to areas of low water concentration (high salinity).

Water is much denser than air, and the water pressure surrounding a marine organism can be extreme. Each 33 feet (10 m) of depth in the ocean adds the equivalent weight of the entire atmosphere at sea level. So that they are not crushed, many simple organisms, such as worms, crustaceans, and sea cucumbers, contain no gases so the pressure inside and outside their bodies is the same.

Remarkably, some marine mammals make long, deep dives but their lungs do not collapse. These animals have many adaptations for deep diving. Before the dive, they take deep breaths, allowing their blood and muscles to absorb oxygen. During the dive, blood is directed to flow only through their brains and hearts. Their lungs collapse completely, so that they contain no gas. Their bodies can go a long time without fresh oxygen and can tolerate high carbon dioxide.

In the photic zone, marine organisms use a variety of strategies to hide from predators. Transparent animals such as jellies blend in with the water. Brown or gray animals are common in murky water. Fish that swim near the sea surface may be black on their topsides and light colored on their undersides to blend in with the bottom when seen from above and with the surface when seen from below. Coral-reef organisms are brightly colored to help them hide near reefs. **Coral reefs** are rich ecosystems surrounding masses of calcium carbonate (limestone) made from coral and other organisms. Color sends a warning to predators that a fish may taste bad, have sharp spines, or be poisonous. Color can be used as protection in another way. For example, a false eyespot on a fish's tail may confuse a predator so that it attacks the animal's tail and not its head.

Darkness makes it easier for organisms to hide from predators, but it also makes it difficult for organisms to find prey or attract mates. Many organisms in the aphotic zone produce light by **bioluminescence**, which is the same chemical reaction that is used by fireflies.

Some organisms have light-producing organs on their sides or on other portions of their bodies.

To see in the dark, marine mammals use a process called **echolocation**. The animal emits sounds of different frequency—low-frequency clicks locate distant objects while higher-frequency clicks determine the sizes and shapes of nearby objects. The clicks bounce off the objects and return to the sender, which helps the animal to build a picture of its environment.

THE MARINE FOOD WEB

Each organism in the sea plays a role in the marine food web. As on land, food energy is created by photosynthetic plants. Food-making organisms are called **producers,** and the food energy they produce is known as **primary productivity**. Amazingly, the ocean is home to a type of producer not found on land. This producer engages in a process called **chemosynthesis**. Chemosynthetic organisms break down chemicals for energy and are found only at hydrothermal vents. The contribution of these organisms to global primary productivity is tiny compared with the contribution of photosynthetic organisms.

Organisms that cannot make their own food and must eat other plants or animals are **consumers**. Some marine consumers are **grazers** that eat plants directly; others are **predators** that hunt other animals for food. **Scavengers** eat dead organic material. Completing the marine food web are **decomposers**, which are usually bacteria. (**Bacteria** are microscopic, single-celled organisms that are not plants or animals; they are members of their own kingdom.) Decomposers use powerful enzymes to break down body parts and waste material into nutrients that can be used by plants or animals. Without decomposers, life on the Earth could not exist because nutrients would not be recycled.

The amount of living matter, or **biomass**, of primary producers is enormous compared to the biomass of the animals that consume them. Also, the number of consumers decreases with each step up the food chain. Predators at the top of the food chain are represented by the smallest number of animals. The biomass decrease occurs because only about 10% of the energy that an organism consumes is stored in its flesh and so can be utilized by the organism that eats it. Therefore, 22,000 pounds (10,000 kilograms) of primary producers will support 2,200 pounds (1,000 kg) of zooplankton, which will support 220 pounds (100 kg) of small fish, which will support about 22 pounds (10 kg) of medium-sized fish, which will support 2.2 pounds (1 kg) of a top predator, such as a tuna.

VARIATIONS IN PRIMARY PRODUCTIVITY

Marine productivity varies regionally and seasonally. Nutrients are most abundant in 1/10 of 1% of the ocean's surface, but those nutrients support about 50% of all marine fishes. In the nutrient-rich polar regions, light is limiting. After a long, dark winter, the arrival of sunlight in spring stimulates a phytoplankton bloom, which supports a rich and diverse food web. In the Southern Ocean, an enormous number of fish and whales feed in the cold, rich waters, some migrating thousands of miles to do so.

In the tropics, where daylight is always available, the warm surface waters rarely allow upwelling, so nutrients are limiting. Without nutrients there are few plants, which is why tropical waters are very blue (phytoplankton-rich waters are green). However, in tropical regions where there is upwelling, such as along the eastern sides of continents and near the equator, life is prolific. Coral reefs, which obtain nutrients from the nearby coasts, are full of life.

In the mid-latitudes, climate and day length are both variable. Winter days are short, so productivity is low. Surface water temperatures decrease, so upwelling brings nutrients to the surface. As daylight increases in spring, productivity increases rapidly.

HOW MARINE ORGANISMS LIVE

The incredible diversity of habitats available in the ocean supports an enormous variety of organisms. How organisms feed, what they eat, and where they live contribute to the diversity of marine life.

Benthic plants and animals are found on the seafloor or in its sediments. The wide range of habitats in and on the sediments has led to the evolution of 150,000 species of benthic animals. All are **invertebrates**—creatures that do not have backbones. Invertebrates are soft-bodied but may have a hard outer covering, like a shell, for protection. Benthic animals include **epifauna** that live on the sea bottom and **infauna** that live buried in soft sediments or that bore into the rocky bottom.

Benthic organisms have a great number of feeding strategies. **Filter feeders** sieve (sift) particles of food from the passing water. **Deposit feeders** eat sediment, digesting the organic material and excreting the rest, and **detritus feeders** eat decomposed plants. Some animals (for example, crabs, starfish, and snails) move along the bottom grazing on seaweed, scavenging for dead animals and plants, or hunting. Scavengers and carnivores also live in the sediments.

Pelagic animals live entirely in the water; most are active swimmers. Many **vertebrates**, which are animals with backbones, have specialized muscles that allow them to swim with or against the current. Some larger invertebrates, such as large jellies and squid, can also direct their movements. The ranges of pelagic animals are restricted by the temperature and salinity characteristics of the water. Fish, squid, marine mammals, and birds that swim in the sea are among the 3,000 species of pelagic swimmers.

Plants and animals must leave behind offspring for the survival of their species. There are many different ways of being reproductively successful. One, which is practiced by invertebrates and fish, is to produce tens of thousands to millions of eggs. This strategy works for animal species in which virtually none of the young survive to reproduce: The eggs and young animals are eaten, the young are unable to compete for resources with older animals or other species, or the mature animals do not successfully mate. The other strategy, pursued by marine mammals and other higher organisms, is to produce a small number of offspring, but to care for them until they are nearly full grown. In this way, the young are more likely to reach maturity and to reproduce.

MARINE ORGANISMS

Some of the many different types of marine organisms are discussed in the following section.

Bacteria

Bacteria are the smallest known and most diverse living organisms. Marine bacteria are found throughout the oceans—in and on every available surface. Each gallon of seawater contains 100 million bacteria, in all depths and latitudes. Marine bacteria can be producers, like those that practice chemosynthesis at hydrothermal vents. They can also be consumers or decomposers, breaking down organic matter into nutrients that can be used by plants. Most bacteria are aerobic oxygen breathers, but some are anaerobic, breaking down compounds such as sulfate to get oxygen. If there were no anaerobic bacteria, the organic material that fell into oxygen-poor waters would not decompose and its nutrients would be lost. Over time, there would be no nutrients left to support life.

Seaweeds and Seagrasses

Seaweeds are multicellular benthic **algae** that need light for photosynthesis. The plantlike organisms attach to the seafloor; their leaves float near the surface, collecting light and nutrients. Seaweeds are very good primary producers and support rich ecosystems. Sea grasses are true plants with leaves for photosynthesis, stems for structure, roots for extracting nutrients, and flowers and seeds for reproduction. Sea grasses commonly form submerged meadows that are home to large and diverse communities of animals.

Plankton

Made of only one or a few cells, tiny plankton cannot swim, but float with the currents. Some are able to move vertically at different times of day to utilize light or avoid predators. Phytoplankton are responsible for around 50% of the primary productivity on the Earth. Many are single or multicelled photosynthesizing algae. Zooplankton eat phytoplankton and are the most abundant consumers in the ocean.

Although zooplankton cannot swim long distances, many can move rapidly to escape predators or to pursue prey. Some zooplankton are animals in their larval stage.

Invertebrates

Invertebrate life reaches its zenith in the oceans. It seems that every microhabitat has a species of marine invertebrate that is adapted to live within it, thus making the numbers and the diversity of marine invertebrates astounding.

Sponges are filter feeders that live attached to the seafloor at all depths and all latitudes. Sponges are theoretically immortal, since if one is broken apart, each of the pieces can become a new animal. **Jellies** are graceful zooplankton with bodies that can be the size of a large bucket, with up to 26 feet (8 m) of tentacles. Jellies sting their prey, injecting them with toxins found at the ends of their tentacles.

The three main types of worms found in the ocean are flatworms, roundworms, and segmented worms. Some are deposit feeders and others are parasites. Tube-dwelling polycheat worms, with tops like feather dusters, are common members of hydrothermal vent-site communities.

Each of the 80,000 species of **mollusks** has an external or internal shell. Mollusks include clams, snails, abalones, limpets, octopuses, and squid. Some mollusks propel themselves through the water with their head and foot projecting out from their coiling shell. Others have two shells that they can open to feed or close for protection. Octopuses have an internal shell; they like to live alone, hiding behind rocks and in cracks. To avoid predators, octopuses can change color for camouflage or can change shape to fit into tiny spaces. When hiding does not work, the animals squirt black ink to distract predators while they escape. The 65-foot (20 m) long giant squid has 10 arms, two that are long, thin tentacles with suckers. Squid can change color or can bioluminesce when necessary. Many have bioluminescent lures to attract prey and use ink to confuse predators.

Marine **arthropods** include **crustaceans** such as krill, copepods, crabs, lobsters, and shrimp. **Krill** have the greatest biomass of any multicellular creature on the Earth. About 2.3 inches (6 centimeters)

A large sea anemone and many sea stars in a tide pool represent just a small amount of the diversity of marine invertebrates. *(© Daniel W. Gotshall/Visuals Unlimited)*

long, these zooplankton are extremely important to the diets of many marine fish, mammals, and birds. **Copepods** are also an important food source for larger animals.

Echinoderms include sea stars, brittle stars, sea urchins, sand dollars, and sea cucumbers. Echinoderms are found clinging to the seafloor at all ocean depths and in nearly all water temperatures. Sea stars can use their powerful feet to open a clamshell and eat the animal inside. Echinoderms may also be filter or deposit feeders.

VERTEBRATES

There are nearly 50,000 species of vertebrates on the Earth. By far the most successful marine vertebrates, for both number and diversity, are the fish.

Fish

Fish inhabit all depths of all oceans, although they are more abundant in surface waters, shallow coastal areas, estuaries, and upwelling zones where there is more food. The two major types of fish are cartilaginous and bony.

Sharks—primitive, ancient, cartilaginous fish—are diverse, successful, and widespread. Sharks have remained nearly unchanged in physiology for 70 million years. Sharks feed on fish, rays (also cartilaginous fish), seabirds, sea turtles, marine mammals, invertebrates, and other sharks. They are quick and efficient predators with keen senses including eyesight, hearing, taste, and electrical sense. Sharks shred their captured prey with up to seven rows of overlapping, serrated teeth. Fortunately, shark attacks on humans are rare. Sharks are hierarchical and social animals. Some sharks lay eggs and others give birth.

Bony fish are far more plentiful and diverse than sharks. Their body shapes determine the environment in which they live and their behavior. Streamlined fish, such as tuna and mackerel, are fast predators, while flat fish, including sole and halibut, peer up from their protected positions on the seafloor. Elongate fish, such as eels, squeeze into spaces between and under rocks. Most fish travel in schools ranging in size from a few fish to groups that cover several square miles. Schooling provides protection for the fish because each fish has less chance of being eaten. Schooling also keeps potential mates together. The most abundant fish are the herring-type fish, which include sardines, anchovies, menhaden, and herring. These small fish feed on zooplankton and are food for other, larger fish, including mackerel, swordfish, and tuna.

Marine Birds

Marine birds inhabit the air and sea. Some live on land while others come ashore only to nest. The wandering albatross (*Diomedea exulans*), with its 11-foot (3.5 m) wingspan, spends four to five years at sea before it is old enough to reproduce. Some marine birds migrate thousands of miles between their feeding area and nesting grounds.

The Wilson's petrel (*Oceanites oceanicus*) is a small, swallowlike bird that flies from pole to pole twice each year.

Avian adaptations for life in a marine environment include such attributes as webbed feet for swimming; long legs for wading; fat deposits, light bones, and air sacs for buoyancy; an oily secretion for waterproofing feathers and providing insulation; highly developed eyesight for locating fish in the water; and a salt gland over the eye to eliminate excess salt. To stay warm, seabirds have high metabolic rates, so they must eat a lot of fish, squid, egg masses, benthic animals, and dead organisms. Diving birds exhale all the air from their lungs and air sacs, shape themselves like torpedoes, and plummet into the sea to catch fish. Skimmers (*Rynchops* sp.) fly with their lower bill in the water and capture anything they encounter. Frigatebirds (*Fregata* sp.) steal food from other seabirds.

Shorebirds are migratory and may be present in groups of up to hundreds of thousands at certain times of the year. Each species of shorebird eats a different type of food depending on the length of its neck, bill, and legs. Herons and egrets, with long legs and necks, wade into deep water and strike at small fish. Sandpipers use their bills to probe the sand and mud for worms and other infauna. Ducks, terns, and gulls probe near the shore for food.

Marine Reptiles

There are few species of marine reptiles, and all but one live in tropical and subtropical waters. Like terrestrial reptiles, marine reptiles are scaly, air-breathing, ectotherms, but they have glands to concentrate and eliminate excess salt.

Sea turtles graze on algae and grasses, although some are meateaters. These include the Atlantic leatherback (*Dermochelys coriacea*), which can be 6.5 feet (2m) long and weigh 1,300 pounds (600 kg). Sea turtles can navigate for long distances and return to the beach where they were hatched to lay their eggs, even after more than 20 years. Marine crocodiles are ancient creatures that live in salt water, primarily swamps and reef islands in tropical waters. They hunt at night, usually in packs, and rip apart their prey. Sea snakes are extremely poisonous; they hunt on shallow slopes and coral reefs, swimming slowly but effectively, using their flattened tails for propulsion.

Marine Mammals

Like land mammals, marine mammals are air-breathing endotherms to which their mothers give birth and nurse. For life in the sea, marine mammals have many adaptations:

- For swimming: streamlined bodies, with slippery skin or sleek hair, and specially adapted limbs
- For warmth: a high metabolic rate and a large surface area-to-volume ratio, few capillaries in their skin so they lose less heat; layers of fat and fur for insulation
- For high salinity: marine mammals swallow little water during feeding, have skin that is impervious to water, and kidneys that excrete concentrated, very saline urine.

All 90 species of **cetaceans**—whales, dolphins, and porpoises—spend their entire lives at sea. They range in size from 6 feet (1.8 m) to 110 feet (33 m) and weigh up to 110 tons (100,000 kg). Whales are intelligent with large, complex brains. They are able to communicate and have complex family and social groupings. Whales use the Sound Fixing and Ranging (SOFAR) channel, a layer of water at a depth of about 3,300 feet (1,000 m) that has excellent temperature, salinity, and pressure conditions for transmitting sound over long distances. Most likely, whales use this communication channel for mating, feeding, and other social functions.

The two main types of whales are toothed and baleen. The 67 species of toothed whales, which include killer whales (*Orchinus orca*), sperm whales (*Physeter macrocephalus*), dolphins, and porpoises, are hunters. Toothed whales use echolocation to create a picture of their environment. Besides using sounds for socializing, toothed whales make loud noises to stun, debilitate, or even kill their prey. Dolphins and porpoises are small-toothed whales. Dolphins are found worldwide—in every ocean and sea and in all temperatures of water. In the open ocean, they travel in large schools at high speeds, eating all kinds of fish. Dolphins are very social, and their pods range in size from a few to up to 500 members. Porpoises also live in all oceans, but mostly near the shore. Although they are similar to dolphins, they live in small social groups and are less acrobatic.

The 11 species of baleen whales filter krill and other zooplankton from seawater using the coarse, fibrous baleen that lines their mouths. Baleen whales include blue whales (*Balaenoptera musculus*) and humpback whales (*Megaptera novaeangliae*). Blue whales are the largest animals that have ever lived: At 100 feet (30 m) long and 165 tons (150,000 kg) in weight, they must eat 6,600 pounds (3,000 kg) of krill each day. Blue whales communicate over enormous areas. Many baleen whales migrate thousands of miles annually. Humpback whales spend summers eating the bountiful plankton in the waters off Antarctica and migrate to warmer waters off Australia and Fiji in winter.

Pinnipeds—seals, sea lions, and walruses—feed in the water but come ashore to mate, raise young, and socialize. Pinnipeds can be found from the tropics to the polar seas on rocky beaches, ice floes, or in caves. Seals have torpedo-shaped bodies, smooth heads, no external ears, and short coarse hair without soft underfur. Seals are graceful swimmers, but they wriggle around awkwardly on land. Some seals migrate long distances. Elephant seals (*Mirounga* sp.) are the largest seals, up to 21 feet (6.5 m) long and weighing 7,780 pounds. (3,530 kg). These giants can dive deeper than any other air-breathing vertebrate, up to 5,120 feet (1,560 m). Like seals, sea lions are streamlined, but they have longer necks, ears and broad front flippers. Sea lions have a soft underfur and move more easily on land.

Although walrus (*Odobenus rosmarus*) can weigh up to two tons, they can rotate their hind flippers to haul themselves out of the water, walk on hard surfaces, and even glide over the sea bottom as if on sled runners. Walrus locate clams with their heavy, muscular whisker pads. With their mouths, they dig the animals up, crush their shells, remove the meat, and spit out the inedible fragments.

A baby manatee swimming at Homossassa Springs, Florida. *(Kike Calvo/V&W/The Image Works)*

Sea otters (*Enhydra lutris*) are the smallest of the marine mammals, rarely exceeding 4 feet (120 cm) in length. Sea otters have no blubber; instead, they have the densest, warmest fur of any animal, with hair more than six times as dense as that found on a human head, about one million hairs per square inch (6.5 square cm). To stay warm, sea otters must eat one-quarter of their body weight each day. Food sources include abalone, clams, seaweed, snails, mussels, crabs, fish, and sea urchins. Sea otters usually live alone; females and males come together only to mate.

Manatees (*Trichechus* sp) and dugongs (*Dugong dugon*) live in warm, tropical waters. These slow-moving animals graze on sea grasses and can consume 10% to 15% of their body weight each day. Both animals are enormous, up to 9 feet (3 m) in length and weighing up to 1,900 pounds (860 kg). Manatees and dugongs are gentle animals that may live to be 50 to 80 years of age. They produce few offspring over their lives. Manatees are solitary, but dugongs can live in herds of 100 to 200 animals. The roughly 2,500 Florida manatees (a subspecies of the West Indian species *Trichechus manatus*) that live in the United States winter in Florida but may migrate along the Gulf Coast or Atlantic Coast in summer. Due to their large size, they have no natural predators. Florida manatees live in shallow, slow-moving rivers, canals, estuaries, bays, and coastal areas.

WRAP-UP

There is no habitable environment in the oceans that does not have a plant or animal living in it. Both the quantity and diversity of marine life are astonishing. Phytoplankton, the sea's main primary producers, and zooplankton are the base of a varied food web. Marine invertebrates have the greatest diversity, living in all depths and environments. Fish are also very diverse, living alone or in schools, sheltered or roaming the seas, at the surface or near the bottom. Marine mammals may live in the water full time or may spend part of their time on land. Bacteria complete the circle of marine life by breaking down tissues and waste products to recycle nutrients for plants and animals to use.

Marine Communities

Marine biology is not only the study of the organisms that live in the ocean environment, but also the study of the communities in which the organisms live. Most marine organisms reside near the shore, where nutrients and light are abundant. Early oceanographers thought that the deep sea was devoid of life, but have since discovered rich ecosystems there. The following exploration of some marine communities starts at the shore, moves into deeper water, and ends at the deep ocean floor.

THE INTERTIDAL

The **intertidal zone** is the sometimes submerged region between the highest high tide and the lowest low tide. These incredibly productive and diverse communities include tide pools, salt marshes, mangrove swamps, and coral reefs. (A **mangrove** is a large flowering tree that grows in dense forests along tropical coasts and sometimes has its roots submerged.) Intertidal zones may be rocky or sediment-covered places like beaches. Because beach sands are constantly shifting, thus preventing organisms from taking hold, burrowing animals such as crabs, clams, and worms are common in these areas. Shorebirds, including sandpipers, seagulls, and pelicans, live on or near the beaches.

Life in the rocky intertidal is harsh, but intertidal organisms are well adapted to the environment. The pounding waves and the variable conditions produced by the ebb and flow of the tides expose organisms to rapid changes in temperature, salinity, moisture, pH, dissolved oxygen, and food supply. High up, where they are usually exposed to air, organisms must protect themselves from the pounding waves, from drying out, and from predation by land animals and birds. The animals who are lower in the intertidal, where they are mostly submerged, must cope with different predators. Tide pools are water-holding basins in rocks in the intertidal and are home to many of the animals of the lower intertidal. Environmental conditions in tide pools are variable due to evaporation, rainfall, and solar heating.

COASTAL WETLANDS

Coastal wetlands are covered all or part of the time with salt water. The water does not move much, so sediment accumulates, providing soil for plants to grow. These habitats supply food, living space, and nurseries for up to 90% of marine fish and shellfish.

A river meets the sea at an **estuary**. Conditions are variable due to the mixing of fresh and salt water, yet estuaries are extremely biologically productive because they are rich in nutrients that run off the land. Fish and shrimp use estuaries as nurseries; salmon pass through estuaries on their way to their spawning grounds.

Mangroves are large evergreen trees whose roots must be covered with salt or brackish water for all or part of the day while never being completely submerged. These arched and interconnected roots trap sediment, which builds up the land surface and allows other plants to colonize the area. The intertwined roots of mangroves provide stability to areas that might be damaged by storms. They also protect against coastal erosion. Fiddler crabs, worms, snails, oysters, and

A mangrove forest in the Florida Everglades with a Great Blue Heron.
(© age footstock/SuperStock)

other invertebrates find safety among the intertwined roots. Birds and insects live in the leaves. Snakes, crabs, and crocodiles move about on the forest floor. Fish, including commercially valuable species, use mangroves as nurseries.

SUBMERGED COMMUNITIES

Further down the shore are communities of organisms that live submerged all, or nearly all, of the time. Sea grass meadows thrive in the soft sediments of bays and estuaries, and off beaches. Like salt marsh grasses, their intertwined roots and dense leaves and stems create a rich habitat for aquatic animals, providing protection from predators and shelter from currents and waves. These environments are extremely productive and are home to large and varied communities of animals. Every major group of animals is represented here. Mobile animals, like snails, crabs, and fish, cruise through the leaves. Migrating birds also use sea grass beds, and raptors, such as eagles, hunt on them. Large vertebrates, like green turtles and manatees, forage and live in sea grass meadows.

Kelp is an extraordinary seaweed that grows in tall, flowing forests up to 130 feet (40 m) high. Kelp can grow up to a foot (30 cm) in a single day. These algae are anchored in the sediments, but their tops are kept at the surface by gas-filled floats so that they can photosynthesize. Kelp forests are good homes for snails, abalone, urchins, and other grazers that are eaten by fish, starfish, and sea otters that in turn are then hunted by sharks, sea lions, and crabs. Kelp forests also serve as habitat for scavengers that consume the dead tissue of other organisms.

Kelp forest off the California coast. *(Gregory Ochocki/Photo Researchers)*

CORAL REEFS

Coral reef ecosystems are among the most spectacular and beautiful ecosystems on the Earth. They harbor more than one-fourth of all marine plant and animal species, or about one million species in all.

Reefs are built of tiny coral animals called **polyps** that construct calcium carbonate ($CaCO_3$) shells around their bodies. When the larva from a young coral polyp attaches itself to a good spot, usually on an existing coral, and builds a shell, the reef grows. A single reef may grow over millions of years and may become hundreds of yards (meters) thick. The world's largest reef, the Great Barrier Reef of Australia, is 1,250 miles (2,000 km) long.

Coral reef in the Florida Keys National Marine Sanctuary. *(Florida Keys National Sanctuary)*

The coral polyps enjoy a mutually beneficial relationship with minute algae (dinoflagellates) called **zooxanthellae**. (A relationship between two species of organisms in which both benefit and neither is harmed is known as **symbiosis**.) In this relationship, the photosynthetic algae supply oxygen and food to the corals, and the corals provide a home and nutrients (coral waste) for the zooxanthellae. The algae give corals their bright colors of pink, yellow, blue, purple, and green. Coral polyps sometimes feed by capturing and eating plankton that drift into their tentacles.

Coral can thrive only in a restricted set of conditions. Water must be warm, but not hot, and fairly shallow with moderately high but constant salinity. The zooxanthellae must have clear, well-lit water to photosynthesize.

Tropical corals are the most common and the most visible, but corals also grow on seamounts in cold, deep water. Deepwater corals grow tall, up to 33 feet (10 m), and are found as deep as 2.2 miles (3.5 km). North Atlantic reefs shelter as many as 1,300 invertebrate and 850 coral species, many of them unique to the ecosystem. Upwelling currents bring up nutrients, providing the materials for a rich food web. These coral polyps are filter feeders, since they live in the aphotic zone. Cold-water reefs are slow growing and can be more than 1,000 years old. Deep reefs provide nurseries and habitats for many important deep-sea species, including commercially valuable fish.

MID-LEVEL AND DEEP-SEA COMMUNITIES

Most mid-level and deep-sea communities rely on food from the sea surface since there is no light for photosynthesis. Many species of deposit-feeding infauna and filter-feeding epifauna live at all levels of the aphotic zone. Large numbers of fish live in the middle levels of the ocean. Some of them come up into the photic zone to feed and then retreat down into the aphotic zone to escape predators. Some evade predators because their silvery color blends into the shimmering water. Some species, like hatchet fish (*Argyropelecus aculeatus*), have enormous eyes to make the best of the available light. Many marine mammals also inhabit the mid-levels of the ocean; they may feed there or at the surface. Some mid- and deep-sea animals are mysterious, such as large squid that are rarely spotted.

The deep sea has no plants, but many kinds of animals are present, even in the deepest of deep-sea trenches, where eyeless snails roam. The number of individuals of each species in the deep sea is small, as is their size due to the scarcity of food. Fish of the deep sea are very specialized. To survive where there is little chance of meeting up with something to eat, these animals move slowly and do not lose an opportunity to capture prey. Most are fierce, even monstrous, in appearance but only between 1 and 12 inches (2 and 30 cm) in length. They use their food for the energy they need to live, with little left for growth. Deep-sea fish breathe slowly and have minimal bone structure and a relatively slow metabolism. To capture their prey, a few species have gaping mouths with jaws that unhinge in case a larger fish is the meal.

To keep the prey from escaping, some have large backwards-folding teeth. Others have a bioluminescent structure projecting from their heads that looks like a fishing lure. Some use bioluminescence to attract mates in the dark.

HYDROTHERMAL VENT COMMUNITIES

Hydrothermal vents are the only mid- or deep-sea communities that produce their own food. Too deep and dark for photosynthesis, they are the only communities on the Earth in which chemosynthesis provides

Hydrothermal Vent Biologist: Cindy Lee Van Dover

Cindy Lee Van Dover has done something no other marine scientist has done. Most deep-sea researchers have been down in the manned submersible *Alvin*, but Van Dover wanted to better understand the deep ocean. While she was becoming a research scientist, she took a major diversion and spent a few years as an *Alvin* pilot.

Van Dover became interested in science in the summer of 1970 when, as a high school junior, she took an advanced marine biology field course, working in the Shellfish Research Lab at Rutgers University.

At that time, women scientists were rare. Van Dover was not encouraged to pursue science by her parents (who humored her) or her guidance counselor (who told her she was not college material). But Van Dover prevailed, receiving an undergraduate degree in

zoology from Rutgers University and a Ph.D. in biological oceanography from Woods Hole Oceanographic Institution in Massachusetts. For her doctoral dissertation research, the young scientist studied the eyeless shrimp that live at some Atlantic hydrothermal vent sites. The shrimp were assumed to be blind because they live far beneath the photic zone. Amazingly, Van Dover discovered a light-sensitive patch, called a *photoreceptor*, on their heads. While trying to figure out what purpose a photoreceptor would serve in the deep sea, Van Dover discovered that hydrothermal vents emit light, mostly in wavelengths that are invisible to humans.

After finishing her doctorate, instead of immediately becoming a professor, Van Dover decided to become an *Alvin* pilot. Pilot training turned out to be far more difficult than her scientific training.

the bulk of the food energy. Hydrothermal vent communities support a typical food web, in which some animals, like snails, eat the bacteria, and some, like fish, consume the animals that eat the bacteria. Other animals live symbiotically with the bacteria. In one symbiotic vent relationship, chemosynthetic bacteria live within the tissues of giant tube worms (*Riftia pachyptila*); the bacteria provide the worms with a constant source of food and, in return, are given shelter.

Hydrothermal vents are incredibly harsh environments for life. The fluids are very acidic (with a pH as low as 2.8); they emit poisonous gases and toxic metals. Fluid temperatures can be up to 750°F

Since *Alvin's* mother ship spends most of its time hundreds or thousands of miles out at sea, pilots must be prepared to fix the sub when necessary. Pilots-in-training spend countless hours studying schematics; pilot certification includes intensive oral exams. Van Dover has been on over 100 *Alvin* dives and was pilot-in-command on 48 of them.

From the *Alvin's* tiny window, she viewed nearly all the known hydrothermal vent fields in the Atlantic and Pacific and many other significant seafloor features. Like all research scientists, she has published many scholarly articles; she has even shared her knowledge more widely by writing the first textbook on hydrothermal vent life. Unlike most scientists, the former *Alvin* pilot has also authored a book for a lay audience about her experiences, *The Octopus's Garden*, in addition to many articles. Van Dover is

Dr. Cindy Lee Van Dover after a dive in *Alvin*, which appears in the background. *(Jenny Paduan)*

now the director of the Duke University Marine Laboratory in North Carolina, and she continues to study hydrothermal vent life.

(400°C) but grade into frigid seawater. Yet the vents are home to more than 300 species, nearly all of them unique to vent sites, such as giant clams (*Calyptogena magnifica*) and eyeless shrimp (*Rimicaris exoculata*). In the nearly three decades since hydrothermal vents were discovered, the vents and their unusual creatures have been the subject of intensive research by scientists.

WRAP-UP

Unlike food webs on land, food webs in the oceans have two sources of energy: photosynthesis and chemosynthesis. Both of these types of energy support varied communities of organisms, such as eyeless shrimp and giant tube worms at hydrothermal vents, coral polyps and brightly colored fish at shallow reefs, and large fast-moving fish and marine mammals in the mid-levels, to name just a few. The oceans provide an important home for life on the Earth.

PART TWO

MARINE RESOURCES

Energy, Mineral, and Nonextractive Resources

Humans use an enormous number and type of resources that are found in the sea, including energy and mineral resources. Much of the energy needed to fuel modern society, mostly as fossil fuels, comes from under the seafloor. Fresh water is processed from seawater in desalination plants. Marine resources also include commodities that are valuable but that remain an inherent part of the ocean or seashore—commodities such as beauty, recreational potential, and shipping.

THE INTERNATIONAL LAW OF THE SEA

Resource use is regulated by the International Law of the Sea. During World War II (1939–1945), a country was considered to own three miles (5 km) of the ocean adjacent to its shore. The rest of the ocean was "free to all and belonging to none." After World War II, some nations began to annex their entire continental shelves to have exclusive access to their resources, especially petroleum. The first coordinated international policy, the Law of the Sea, was formulated by the United Nations (UN) in 1982 and came into force in 1994. This law regulates all aspects of the use of the ocean including navigation, resource management, environmental protection, and marine research.

The Law of the Sea states that a nation owns its territorial waters up to 12 miles (18 km) from shore. Up to 200 nautical miles (370 km) out is a nation's **Exclusive Economic Zone (EEZ)**, in which it has sovereign rights to both living and nonliving resources, economic activity, and environmental protection. Forty percent of the ocean falls within some nation's EEZ. The remaining 60% is in the high seas, which are the common property of all the world's citizens. In total, EEZs hold about 87% of oil and gas reserves and the best fisheries.

The Law of the Sea has been approved by virtually all special interest groups (military, industry, fishing, foreign trade, and environmental) in the United States. However, the United States has signed but not ratified the treaty because it finds the provisions too restrictive on many grounds. As a signatory, the United States recognizes its own EEZ, totaling 4 million square miles (10.3 million square km), nearly 25% more area than the nation's total land area. This region, the largest ocean jurisdiction of any country in the world, is extremely rich in natural resources, including petroleum and natural gas deposits located off Alaska, California, and within the Gulf of Mexico; hydrothermal vents with their sulfide chimneys off the Pacific Northwest; and manganese nodules off the Atlantic and Pacific coasts, Hawaii, and Pacific Island territories.

FOSSIL FUELS

The word *fossil* in the term *fossil fuels* is a reminder that petroleum, coal, and natural gas are made of the remains of ancient organisms. The energy of these fuels is ancient solar energy that plants converted into food energy by photosynthesis and that remained in the organisms' bodies when they died. Fossil fuels are **nonrenewable resources**; that is, natural processes do not replenish them on a timescale that is useful for humans. By contrast, tidal and wave energy are examples of **renewable resources**; they can be used without being completely eliminated.

Petroleum (crude oil) is mostly the remains of plankton that lived millions to hundreds of millions of years ago. After death, the organisms accumulated on the seafloor and were buried by sediments. If they accumulated in a deep, oxygen-free basin, anaerobic bacteria changed their remains into simpler organic compounds. If the temperature reached between 120°F and 300°F (50°C and 150°C), the organic material converted to oil. With deeper burial and hotter temperatures, the organic material converted to methane, the main ingredient in natural gas. Since oil is less dense than the sediments it forms in, the liquid migrates upward through the sediment pores. If the oil encounters a watertight rock layer lying atop a porous one, it becomes trapped in this area and must be drilled and pumped to the surface for use by humans.

Much of the petroleum used today—about 35% of the oil and 26% of the natural gas—comes from the seabed. Most of it is located in the continental margins; there are no known oil reserves in the deep ocean. Most of the offshore deposits that are taken are less than 330 feet (100 m) deep. Collecting this oil is not easy; offshore drilling is expensive and difficult. Drilling must be done from platforms that require specialized drilling equipment and transport systems. The shallow continental shelf of the Gulf of Mexico provides a substantial portion of the oil and natural gas required for the domestic needs of the United States. As the price of oil increases, oil companies are looking for, and finding, deposits farther out on the continental margins, including in the Gulf of Mexico.

The crude oil that is pumped from the ground must be refined before it can be used. This is done by boiling the oil to remove the useful product. The lightest portion of this refined product becomes gasoline for motor vehicles, while heavier products are used for ships and power stations, and still heavier ones are tars. Sometimes materials are added to make the oil useful for other purposes.

METHANE HYDRATES

Methane is also found in ocean sediments as **methane hydrates**. In these compounds, water molecules form an icy cage (a hydrate), which often contains a guest molecule, usually methane. Because the water is not chemically bonded, the cage is unstable and the methane can easily be released and used as fuel. Methane hydrates develop when decomposed organic matter contacts cold water at high pressure, such as when organic matter is buried beneath layers of sediments, a situation found in some continental slope sediments.

There are more deposits of methane hydrates than all the known coal, oil, and nonhydrate natural gas combined, although no one knows exactly how much there is or how much is recoverable. The deposits are found in layers at depths of 660 to 1,650 feet (200 to 500 m) below the seafloor, but most of them are too thin or too far from shore to be economically valuable. Also, because it is unstable, methane hydrate is very difficult to mine. When it is brought up to lower pressures at the surface, the structure collapses, and the methane escapes. The gas burns vigorously if ignited, making it dangerous to work with. Extracting the methane and liquefying it for use would require the development of new technologies and would be very expensive.

Useable gas can be produced from methane hydrates, but experiments so far have been small scale. Some researchers predict that it will be decades before methane hydrates contribute significantly to energy use. Others say that methane production could begin as soon as the mid- to late-2010s and will become significant in a few more decades. If the gas can ever be harnessed, there will be enough methane hydrate to fuel energy needs for at least a few decades, possibly for hundreds or thousands of years.

MINERAL RESOURCES

Mineral resources found in the ocean include metals, gemstones, and materials that are used for fertilizers, in construction, and for many other purposes. Only a small percentage of mineral resources come from the ocean, and those are mostly taken from the continental margins.

Greatest in dollar value are sand and gravel, although only one percent of the total amount mined each year comes from the sea. These substances are used in making cement, concrete, and glass, and for road construction and artificial beaches.

Magnesium is a strong, lightweight metal that is valuable in the aerospace industry, where weight is a concern. Magnesium salts are useful for chemical processes and are used in foods, medicines, soil conditioners, and the linings of high-temperature furnaces. Much of the world's magnesium metal and salts comes from seawater. Magnesium is worth hundreds of millions of dollars to the United States each year.

Salts are created commercially in large, shallow salt ponds in arid regions. The mineral halite (sodium chloride), also known as table salt, is used for salting and preserving food, snow and ice removal, water softeners, agricultural processes, and making soap and glass. Other salts obtained this way include gypsum, used for wallboard and other building materials; potassium salts, a component of some chemicals and fertilizers; bromide, used in some medicines, chemical processes, and anti-knock gasoline; and magnesium salts, used as discussed above. The United States produced about $155 million of table salt in 2001.

More than 95% of manganese is combined with other metals and used in iron and steel manufacture. Although they have not yet been mined, manganese nodules, discussed in Chapter 1, could be an enormous source of this important metal. Early experiments show that mining manganese nodules is feasible but expensive, since the nodules are generally deep and far from shore. As terrestrial manganese deposits are mined out, the mining of manganese nodules is likely.

Phosphorite deposits contain nodules with high concentrations of phosphates, an important component of fertilizers and industrial chemicals. Offshore deposits are currently too expensive to mine, but they may become more attractive as terrestrial deposits become scarcer. The phosphates come from the shells of marine invertebrates and the bones and excrement of vertebrates, such as birds.

Sulfide chimneys, found at hydrothermal vent sites, contain valuable metals such as zinc, iron, copper, lead, silver, and cadmium. Although they are found in deep water usually far from the coast, the deposits may be economically possible to mine in some locations. For example, the Juan de Fuca Ridge, which is off the coast of Oregon and Washington and within the EEZ of the United States, is being studied for its mineral potential.

FRESH WATER

Some people do not have access to clean fresh water, particularly in arid regions. Seawater desalination is becoming increasingly important in some of these locations, including the United States and the countries of the Middle East. According to the American Water Works Association, in 2007 there were more than 15,000 desalination plants in 120 countries, 60% of them located in the Middle East. Desalination provides 70% of the potable water in Saudi Arabia.

About half of the desalination plants boil seawater then condense the water vapor, a process that uses extremely large amounts of energy and is very expensive. The cost is reduced if the energy comes from an electrical power plant that uses seawater for cooling. An increasingly important desalination method is reverse osmosis, in which energy is used to force salt water through an osmotic membrane. The fresh water passes through and the salts remain. In electrodialysis, positive and negative ions are driven through filters by an electric current. After the fresh water is collected, the remaining saline brine must be disposed of properly so that it does not raise the salinity of the nearby ocean to dangerous levels.

MARINE ENERGY

The ocean is alive with the energy of moving water, some of which can be harnessed for use. Tidal energy, for example, uses the rising and falling of the tides. Water is trapped behind a dam-like structure at high tide and released at low tide; the energy of the falling water is collected. Although a few tidal energy plants have been built, the structures are large, expensive, and restrict water movement, causing environmental damage. Waves and currents also contain a lot of energy, but existing technologies to harness them are too expensive.

Ocean thermal energy conversion uses the difference in temperature between warm surface waters and the cold deep waters. Heat from the surface waters vaporizes a fluid with a low boiling point, like ammonia, which turns a generator to produce electricity. Cold deeper water is pumped up to recondense the vapor so the ammonia is conserved. Experiments into this technique have been successful, but it is not very efficient and the plants would be complex to build and expensive to maintain. The technology may become useful to developing island nations in the tropics where the temperature differential in the water is highest; in these areas, the differential makes the technique relatively efficient.

NONEXTRACTIVE RESOURCES

Beautiful scenery, recreational potential, and transportation are some of the nonextractive resources provided by the oceans. Because of their beauty, the availability of recreational activities, and relatively temperate weather, coastlines are popular places for development and tourism. More than one-half of the world's people live within 40 miles (60 km) of the ocean, and the number who do so is increasing all the time. Similarly, more than half of Americans live in counties that border the coast, and even more will be living along the coast by 2010. Coastal tourists spend a great deal of money swimming, fishing, whale watching, surfing, scuba diving, visiting theme parks, and staying in beachfront accommodations. The cost of maintaining coastal development is high. Sand is always on the move and, as a result, beach communities must constantly struggle to keep their property from being damaged or destroyed. Sediments are lost from a beach in several ways: (1) Longshore currents move sand down the beach, (2) offshore currents transport sand away from the beach, and (3) wind blows sand into dunes located inland from the beach.

Sediments are always being added to the beach in several ways, as well: (1) Longshore currents transport sand up the beach, (2) rivers deposit sand and gravel from inland, (3) erosion dumps sand and gravel from beach cliffs, and (4) gentle waves transport sand from offshore. If a beach gains more sand than it loses, it grows. If it loses more sand than it gains, it erodes.

Since development must be protected, people have worked out two rather primitive ways to deal with natural beach processes. One is to interrupt the longshore transport of sand, and the other is to redirect wave energy. Unfortunately, both of these methods have bad side effects.

Groins are solid structures that are built perpendicular to the beach to collect sand on the upstream side of a longshore current. This traps sand for the beach on the upstream side, but starves the beaches on the downstream side. **Jetties** collect sand on the upstream side of a longshore current. They protect the inlets in barrier islands that allow boats to travel from the sea into the lagoon behind. Jetties eventually collect so much sand that they must be dredged or the inlet closes. **Breakwaters** are built parallel to the beach to absorb wave energy, thereby decreasing shore erosion. Since breakwaters interrupt longshore currents, sand accumulates on the up-current side of the breakwater and erosion takes place on the down-current side, again building up one beach at the expense of another. **Seawalls** are built on the edge of a shore to protect structures from storm waves. The structures increase the intensity of rip currents, so more sand is transported seaward. Eventually, a beach with a seawall becomes sand-starved, and the seawall collapses. The seawall at Galveston Island, Texas (a barrier island), is 17 feet (5 m) high; it was built to protect the barrier island from hurricanes after the deadly hurricane of September 1900 that killed between 4,000 and 6,000 people.

Engineers sometimes replenish beaches by trucking in new sand. While this is effective, it is only temporary if the processes that caused the beach to lose sand remain. Trucking in sand is very expensive, and finding clean sand is not always easy.

The ocean is important for recreation: Vacationers flock to the beach to play, to dive, and to fish. Increasingly, they spend their holidays cruising on the sea. A great deal of money is spent on marine recreation. According to the International Council of Cruise Lines,

Dauphin Island, Alabama

Dauphin Island is a 15-mile (24 km) long barrier island that most coastal scientists would agree should never have been developed. The island lies across the opening to Mobile Bay and is regularly breached by coastal storms. Hurricane Frederick knocked out the bridge to the mainland in 1979. At that time, coastal scientists said that the bridge should not be rebuilt and that people should not be allowed to build in hazardous coastal areas. Yet the bridge was rebuilt and, in the intervening years, Dauphin Island has become even more developed.

The temporary truce with the sea was broken when Hurricane Katrina slammed into the Gulf of Mexico coast in August 2005. On the relatively high eastern side of Dauphin Island, some of the beach

Triplet of photos of Dauphin Island. The top image was taken in July 2001 before Hurricane Lili struck in 2002. This photo shows a road and two parallel canals. The middle image was taken on September 17, 2004, just after Hurricane Ivan struck. Sand has covered over the road and the first canal. The bottom image was taken on August 31, 2005, just two days after Hurricane Katrina. Sand covers the road, has filled the first canal, and is encroaching on the second canal. (USGS Coastal & Marine Ecology Program)

(continues)

(continues)

eroded away. Seawalls were broken and tossed into the waves. Even so, the healthy dune system protected much of the area and some houses remained standing. On the lower west side of the island, the dunes had long been eroded away, leaving most houses and the island's roads vulnerable. Houses that were supported by pilings were held up, but other houses collapsed. Sand flowed over the island into the lagoon behind it. "It's as if the island is sliding out from under the houses," Dr. Robert S. Young, a geologist at Western Carolina University, told the *New York Times* in September 2005, as he observed the destruction from the air.

On an undeveloped barrier island, storm waters bring sand over the island and into the lagoon to create new land. The land is colonized by seagrass and a marsh forms. In this way, the barrier island moves landward. People can try to stop these natural processes and may even succeed, but on a piece of land as transient as a barrier island, a hurricane can bring catastrophe to people who lose their homes and, possibly, their lives.

the cruise industry annually accounts for $16 billion in spending in North America, and recreational saltwater fishing has been estimated to be worth $20 billion. The migration of tourist money to the coastal regions increases the development of hotels, restaurants, theme parks, shops, and other vacation necessities.

For thousands of years, travel on the ocean was the only way to quickly move people and goods great distances. Even today, although airplane travel has greatly decreased the number of people who travel by ship, shipping is the least expensive way to move goods, and most globalized trade takes place on the seas. The greatest shipping commodity is oil because most oil fields are in locations far from the populations that use the resource and many oil fields are offshore. Oil tankers as large as 1,300 feet (430 m) long and 206 feet (66 m) wide can carry more than 3.5 million barrels (500,000 metric tons) of oil. According to the United States Commission on Ocean Policy, U.S. ports handle $700 billion worth of goods annually.

Undersea cables have been carrying information across the sea-floor since the nineteenth century and will continue to do so, even as satellite communication becomes more important. Seafloor cables and pipes also carry electricity, oil, and other goods across the oceans.

WRAP-UP

The ocean supplies extractive and nonextractive resources. A large percentage of fossil fuels, and some sand and gravel, come from the continental margins. Desalination plants turn seawater into drinking water for the world's arid lands. Other resources, such as methane hydrates and manganese nodules, hold promise for the future but are currently expensive and difficult to obtain. Nonextractive resources, such as shipping, development, and recreation, may not actually take resources out of the sea, but they are of great economic importance.

Biological Resources

People use an enormous number and varied types of resources that are found in the sea, including energy and mineral resources. This chapter will focus mostly on the oceans' biological resources. Fish and shellfish account for much of the protein that people rely upon. Marine fisheries provide jobs for about 200 million people worldwide—jobs that include the catching, processing, and selling of fish and the manufacture of ships and other equipment. Marine organisms also supply a few of the chemicals used in pharmaceuticals, with the promise of many more discoveries in the future.

SEAWEEDS

Seaweeds have many more uses than most people may realize. Compounds made from seaweed are used in industrial processes, including tire manufacture. Seaweed products are used as thickeners or stabilizers for many products, like ice cream and cosmetics. Red algae are used to wrap rice in China and Japan and are ingredients in bread in parts of the British Isles. Brown seaweed is made into a number of food products and is a good source of vitamins and minerals. Seaweeds can also be used for fertilizer or animal feed.

MARINE FISHERIES

The oceans provide an enormous food resource for the world's people. Marine fish and shellfish are the primary source of protein for one-sixth of the world's population and provide a portion of the protein for many more. Some of this protein comes from **aquaculture**, which is the raising and harvesting of seaweed, fish, and shellfish, but most comes from the wild catch.

Fewer than 500 of the thousands of species of marine animals are harvested for consumption. Finfish make up most of the catch, with mollusks, such as oysters, scallops, and squid, and crustaceans, such as shrimp, lobsters, and krill, filling out nearly all of the rest. People eat much of the harvest, but some of it is made into animal feed, fertilizers, and other products. In the 1950s, 90% of the catch was used for human consumption and 10% as meal for animals. In 2002, 76% was for direct human consumption; the rest was for nonfood products, mainly fishmeal and oil.

Fishing is now a global business. In 1950, about 20 million tons (18 billion kg) of fish and shellfish were harvested globally. Since then, the world's population has tripled and seafood production has increased to 130 million tons (118 billion kg). The incredible increase in the fish harvest was made possible by a tremendous increase in effort, including a doubling of the number of fishing boats between 1970 and 1990. Fishing methods also have become more sophisticated and fleets now find fish by using sound navigation and ranging (**sonar**) vessels, planes, helicopters, and satellites. Fishing has evolved into a more efficient and often more lethal activity.

Net fishing is the most productive, and also the most damaging, way to catch fish. Drift nets were so lethal to marine life that they were banned by a United Nations (UN) resolution in 1992. That year, fishing vessels put out an estimated 30,000 miles (48,000 km) of nets

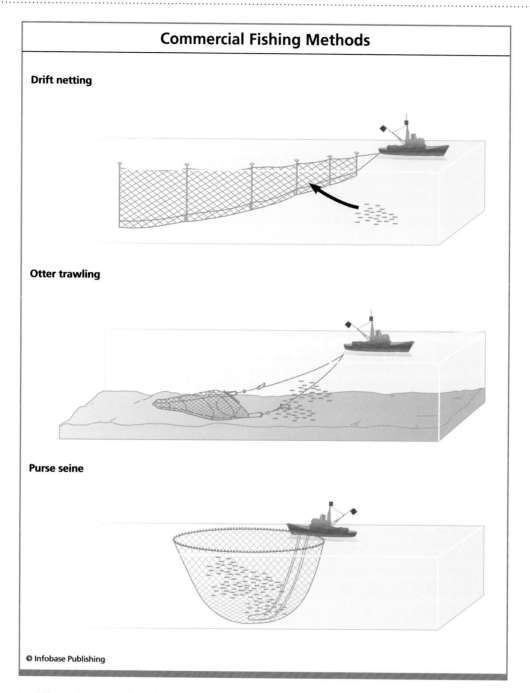

Commercial Fishing Methods

Drift netting

Otter trawling

Purse seine

© Infobase Publishing

In drift netting, a series of nets is hung vertically in the water using floats. Shoals of fish swimming into the netting become trapped by their gills. In otter trawling, a large net, or trawl net, is towed along the seabed by a fishing vessel. Shoals of fish swim directly into the open mouth of the net. In the purse seine method, the fishing vessel detects a shoal of fish, then a large net is quickly run around the entire shoal.

A fisherman in Newfoundland, Canada, empties a cod trap. *(© Eastcott/Momatiuk/ The Image Works)*

each night. Each of these nets drifted like an invisible wall, 40 miles (64 km) long, catching the fish and squid the vessels were after, but also everything else that came into contact with it. Even now, drift nets continue to be illegally put out each night.

In midwater, trawl nets catch large schools of small fish, such as anchovies. Trawl nets are also dragged over the seafloor to catch bottom-dwelling fish, such as cod and halibut. Purse seine nets are set out to encircle a school of fish. The bottom of each net is pulled closed like a purse and when the net is raised, the target fish—usually sardines, herring, mackerel, and tuna—are trapped inside.

Line fishing by commercial fishers is done with a pole or a long-line. Poles are long with short, hooked lines. When fishers catch a fish, they whip the line overhead, unhook the fish instantly, and return the line to the water. This technique is effective for large pelagic fish, such as tuna and mahi-mahi. Longlines stretch up to 50 miles (80 km) long; many smaller lines project outward, each with thousands of hooks. The fish are taken off the line as it is reeled in. Midwater fish such as swordfish and tuna, and bottom fish such as cod, halibut, and sablefish, are caught this way. In trolling, fishers put out a long rod and line behind a moving vessel to attract such speedy fish as salmon, albacore tuna, and mahi-mahi.

Lobster, crabs, shrimp, and bottom-dwelling fish are caught in baited cages, known as traps or pots. The animal goes in for the bait and cannot come out, unless it is undersized. After a few days, the fishers return to collect the trapped, live animals.

Factory ships follow the large fishing fleets and process, can, or freeze the catch immediately. This has made fishing more efficient, as the fishing boats can continue to fish without returning to shore.

Coastal nations are permitted to exploit the fisheries within their Exclusive Economic Zone (EEZ). Forty percent of the ocean falls within some nation's EEZ, and all nations are allowed to fish in the deep sea. In the United States, the federal agency charged with researching and exploiting marine resources is the National Oceanic and Atmospheric Administration (NOAA). Since 1970, NOAA's mandate has been to protect marine life and property from natural hazards, to better understand the marine environment, and to explore and develop marine resources intelligently. One department within NOAA, the National Marine Fisheries Service (NMFS), is designed to protect, study, manage, and restore fish. NOAA's placement in the Department of Commerce is a sign that use of marine resources plays a large role in the agency's mission.

MARINE AQUACULTURE

Although the ocean is extremely productive, rising demand, environmental degradation, and decreasing fish populations are resulting in a decreased catch. To meet demand, fish and shellfish are increasingly grown in the way people raise meat—on farms and ranches. This activity is termed aquaculture.

In 1970, less than 4% of the total production of fish, crustaceans, and mollusks was from aquaculture; in 2006, the percentage was 31%; and by 2030 aquaculture will account for more than half of all fish production, according to statistics from the UN. This is a tremendous increase compared with those of other protein sources. Since 1970, the average annual rise in production by aquaculture has been 8.9%, with only a 1.2% rise for wild fisheries, and a 2.8% rise for land-based farming (beef, chicken, etc.). More than half of the farmed species are freshwater fish, and a large proportion of the aquaculture expansion has been in China. Worldwide, aquaculture is a $50 billion a year industry.

Like farm animals on land, farmed fish must have a safe environment in which to grow, be healthy, and be protected from predators. For a species to be successfully farmed, it must be hearty, inexpensive to feed, and able to reproduce in captivity. Population density is high, so keeping animals healthy and keeping wastes flushed out are priorities.

Saltwater animals can be farmed in earth or concrete ponds, behind barricades, or in cages suspended in water or anchored to the seafloor. The enclosures must be strong enough to survive storms. Currents moving through the cages replace the oxygen and eliminate the waste. For fish that are raised in ponds, population densities are even higher. Therefore, water must be pumped in, and the wastes must be pumped out. Shellfish can be raised on ropes suspended from submerged buoys in deep water with the animals growing on the ropes. In fish ranching, young fish or shellfish are raised in a controlled environment and then released into the open ocean to grow to maturity.

MARINE MAMMALS

Products from marine mammals were once commonplace, and the history of the commercial hunting of these animals is long. Some marine mammals were eaten; others were taken for their luxurious pelts, their oil, or their ivory tusks. Especially popular with hunters were whales, seals, and sea otters.

Indigenous cultures hunted whales for thousands of years, eating the meat, and using the oil for fuel and light, the bones for tools and construction, and the baleen for structural support. European cultures have primarily used whales for oil, although the meat, bones, and baleen were also of use. Whale meat has been popular in Asia at various times and is consumed in some countries even today.

Seals have thick, beautiful fur coats to keep themselves warm in the frigid ocean. People's desire to wear sealskin coats fueled an intense seal-hunting industry. Otters were also hunted for their fur, the thickest fur of any mammal. In the past, manatees and dugongs were hunted for their meat and for their tough skins, which were used

Artificial Reefs

In locations where the seafloor is sandy and organisms cannot gain a foothold, or where there is a recreational need, artificial reefs can be created. To create an artificial reef is fairly simple: Sink a man-made object into a good location. The most commonly used objects are steel-hulled ships or boats and oil platforms, but there are also sunken cars, military tanks, bridges, concrete culvert pipe, aircraft, and even intercontinental ballistic missiles. These objects, which are mostly trash, provide purchase for organisms and quickly become the foundation of a reef ecosystem. Mussels, barnacles, and other marine invertebrates colonize the area; soon, fish find their way to the reef. Barracuda (*Sphyraena* sp.) have been seen staking territory moments after the sunken material lands on the seafloor. Artificial reef communities can be just as productive and varied as natural communities. Artificial reefs also provide locations for recreational fishing and sport diving where none were available or where more are needed. The reef community lasts as long as the reef structure lasts.

Off Southern California, there are currently 27 working oil platforms located between 1.2 and 10.5 miles (2 and 17 km) from shore and in water depths from 35 to 1,200 feet (11 to 366 m). The platforms have unique features that make them extremely suitable for rockfish habitats. Unlike other reefs, natural or artificial, oil platforms provide habitat throughout the water column. This habitat appears to be especially valuable to rockfish, since these animals prefer to live in different water levels at different parts of their life stages. Perhaps this is because predato make boat covers, shoes, and other heavy-duty articles. The animals were also hunted for their fat; their bones and tusks were used for carvings.

CORAL REEFS

Coral reefs are not only important and beautiful ecosystems, they are vital to the economies of some small nations and to the livelihoods of some people. Reef animals are used for food and pharmaceuticals. The reef's structure provides construction materials and decoration. Tourists—divers and snorkelers—love coral reefs and tourism from

tors seek out adults that are living at one level, which allows juveniles, who live at a different water level, more time to develop. Adult rockfish like the platforms for the many sheltered hiding places the structures contain. California's platforms have had, on average, a relatively undisturbed 25 years to develop into mature, diverse, and thriving reef communities that include substantial rockfish populations. Although rockfish are being fished in excess, fishing is not allowed at the platforms, which means they can act as reserves, protecting the fish and allowing their population to grow.

Regulations require that platforms be removed after they are no longer in production, which destroys the habitat for rockfish and other organisms. Where nearby platforms have been removed, many tons of marine organisms have been destroyed. If retired platforms were left in place, they would not only provide habitat for organisms, they could be important tourist diving locations, bringing money into the local economy.

While there are positive features to artificial reefs, it is important that they be constructed in an environmentally safe manner. Reef materials should not be toxic or contain pollutants, and reef construction should not damage natural habitats or displace natural species or habitats. As Jack Sobel, a spokesperson for the Ocean Conservancy in Washington, D.C., told *E Magazine* in 2004, "Artificial reefs can do as much harm as good. They are no replacement for natural reefs or for proper fisheries management, and we don't want people to view the oceans as a dumping ground for our wastes."

reef visitors is important to many local economies. In all, coral reefs are worth an estimated $375 billion each year in economic and environmental services, such as protecting the coastline from storms. Reefs are so important that artificial reefs are sometimes created.

DRUGS FROM THE SEA

To enhance their chance of survival, some organisms manufacture chemicals that make them attractive to mates or deter predators or competitors. A few of these compounds can also be used to manufacture medicines that help to cure or slow the development of human diseases. More than 100 drugs currently on the market come from chemicals that were derived from terrestrial microorganisms, but sources of new terrestrial microbes are dwindling. Finding new antibiotics has become particularly important since many bacteria are becoming resistant to known antibiotic drugs. Of course, new cancer drugs are always needed to fight the many forms of that disease. Because many terrestrial sources have already been exploited, the oceans have become a new and exciting place to search for potential pharmaceuticals.

To look for new drugs from the sea, marine organisms—particularly invertebrates, microorganisms, and algae, all from diverse habitats—are catalogued and then sampled for compounds that kill bacteria or fungi. Marine forms of the terrestrial bacteria that are the source of several antibiotic drugs, including streptomycin, have been discovered in deep-sea sediments. One compound from the same bacteria inhibits cell growth, including that of cancerous tumors such as breast cancer and human colon carcinoma.

Invertebrates produce chemicals that are useful for pharmaceuticals. Because sponges cannot move, they prevent organisms from growing on top of them by secreting a chemical. This chemical keeps the infringing organism from growing by interrupting its cell division and has been shown to be a powerful anticancer drug. The drug is in phase I clinical trials for its ability to arrest the growth of solid tumors, such as those in breast, colon, lung, and other cancers. Another sponge, from the Caribbean, was the source of the first antiviral compound ever used in humans, the drug Acyclovir. A type of toxic algae, *Karenia brevis proliferate*, contains a chemical that is used to treat cystic fibrosis.

WRAP-UP

The oceans supply the global human population with an enormous amount of food. To harvest this food, people have developed a great number of techniques for catching fish and shellfish; some of these methods are deadly to fish populations. Recently, raising animals in fish and shellfish farms has become an important method for increasing the amount of available animal protein. Hunting marine mammals for their oil, fur, and other commodities is an activity that took place largely in the past, although it still goes on at a low level today. Drugs derived from the chemicals produced by marine organisms are a resource that will continue to grow in coming decades.

PART THREE

EFFECTS OF POLLUTION ON THE OCEANS

The Activities
of Pollutants

The oceans provide humans with energy and mineral resources, food, and climate moderation, as well as many other commodities and services. Not only do people take resources from the oceans, they also add materials to them. The ocean is the ultimate sink for the chemical wastes of human society. Although oceans are vast, the expanding human population seems to be rapidly pushing the seas' capacity to absorb some types of waste.

POLLUTANT INPUTS AND OUTPUTS

Pollutants are being added to the ocean in large and ever-increasing amounts. A material is a pollutant if it is found in unnatural quantities or if it is found where it should not be. Pollutants that are not natural to the ocean include plastics and some man-made chemicals. Most substances, including heavy metals, oil, sediments, nutrients, and even radioactivity, are found naturally in the sea in some locations, but in some areas their concentrations are higher due to human activities.

Pollutants enter the ocean from the atmosphere, the land, and directly from industrial or municipal sources. Airborne pollutants rain into the ocean; this is a large source of nitrates, which come from car exhaust. The same pollutants that contaminate streams, lakes, and groundwater also travel in the fresh water to befoul the oceans. Pollutants may also enter the oceans from runoff; for instance, from soil to which pesticides were applied, or from improperly maintained landfills.

Pollutants enter directly into the ocean, as well. **Sewage**, the waste matter that passes through sewers, may enter the ocean either raw or partially treated. Routine ship operations such as discharging ballast water (used to stabilize a ship) and bilge water (a ship's sewage), and discarded litter, which includes many plastics, are responsible for a great deal of marine pollution. Shipwrecks dump oil, heavy metals, plastics, and even everyday objects such as tennis shoes into the ocean.

Pollutants enter the sea every day, but unlike water, they do not evaporate. Some leave the seas by adhering to the tiny clay minerals that fall through the water column and collect on the seafloor, where they are eventually buried by other sediments. Ocean pollutants may also be diluted, dispersed, or degraded. Water from rain, streams, and other sources, which are constantly added to the oceans, dilutes the pollutants. Currents and waves mix the water, causing many pollutants to be diluted to concentrations that are well below harmful levels. Some types of pollutants break down into harmless compounds.

In many places, the sea may have reached its limit on how much pollution it can soak up. The worst pollution is found close to where it is dumped and so the most polluted regions are near shorelines. But no area of the oceans is unaffected: Currents carry pollutants to northern and southern oceans and into the deep sea. Toxic chemicals are found in the bodies of Arctic seals and Antarctic penguins, thousands of miles from where the pollutants were used.

THE BEHAVIOR OF POLLUTANTS

Most pollutants are **biodegradable**; they can be broken down by bacteria into inorganic compounds that are not hazardous, such as CO_2, H_2O, and ammonia. But adding too much biodegradable material to an ecosystem is still harmful since it is like adding fertilizer. Bacteria bloom to consume the material and use up the supply of oxygen, which then is no longer available for other organisms. Anaerobic bacteria may degrade the waste further, producing the byproducts hydrogen sulfide (the source of the rotten-egg smell of rotting waste) and methane, creating an environment that hardly any marine organisms can tolerate. Many pollutants are not biodegradable, but break apart, become chemically altered, or combine with other chemicals to form new compounds that may be harmful.

Animals take in toxic compounds from water, sediment, or food, which may have health effects. In rare cases, a substance may be so toxic that it is fatal in the smallest doses. But most have longer-term effects on health including physiological stress, tumors, or developmental abnormalities such as damage to internal organs, skeletal deformities, erosion of fins, and precancerous growths.

Toxic compounds may undergo **bioaccumulation**; that is, the substance accumulates and becomes more concentrated as it moves up the marine food web. Tiny zooplankton take in a tiny amount of a toxic substance, but the small fish that eat them accumulate all of the substance from all of the zooplankton they eat. Larger fish accumulate all of the toxic substance from all of the small fish they eat, and so on up the food web. Animals in the upper levels of the food web may have enormous concentrations of toxic compounds stored in their body fat. If they metabolize the fat, the toxic compounds enter their systems. Substances that have little noticeable effect in small organisms may cause great damage in large predators. Consuming a daily dose of **mercury**—a heavy metal that is toxic as a liquid, salt, or organic compound—would eventually result in neurological problems and death.

Ocean food chains are longer than terrestrial ones, so top marine predators have higher concentrations of toxic compounds; this is why people are advised to limit their consumption of tuna. The damage to organisms from bioaccumulating pollutants was one of the motivations for the passage of the Endangered Species Act of 1973.

Few pollutants enter the ocean as single substances; and because they often enter mixed with other pollutants, scientists have difficulty

understanding the effects of any one chemical type. Sewage is a domi-
nantly organic material that also includes oil, toxic chemicals, fertilizers
(mostly nitrates and phosphates), pesticides, **pathogens** (disease-causing
organisms), and whatever else may be contained in the water that flows
into sewage.

The damage a toxic substance does to a species differs due to a
variety of factors. For example, if only some individuals are contaminated in a species with high reproductive rates, the species will not

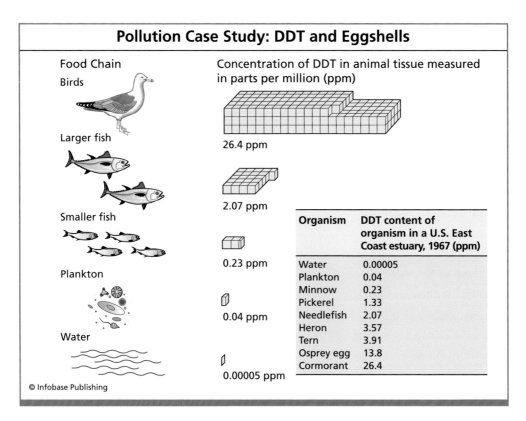

Pollution Case Study: DDT and Eggshells

Food Chain

Birds

Larger fish

Smaller fish

Plankton

Water

Concentration of DDT in animal tissue measured in parts per million (ppm)

26.4 ppm

2.07 ppm

0.23 ppm

0.04 ppm

0.00005 ppm

Organism	DDT content of organism in a U.S. East Coast estuary, 1967 (ppm)
Water	0.00005
Plankton	0.04
Minnow	0.23
Pickerel	1.33
Needlefish	2.07
Heron	3.57
Tern	3.91
Osprey egg	13.8
Cormorant	26.4

© Infobase Publishing

Pollutants can enter the food chain and contaminate living organisms. In the 1960s and
1970s, populations of birds, including such seabirds as brown pelicans and ospreys, were
badly affected by DDT, a pesticide. Here, the route of contamination from polluted water
to fish-eating birds is illustrated. Concentrations of DDT in this example are measured in
parts per million (ppm). Because of DDT's harmful effects on wildlife and the environment,
its use has been banned in the United States since 1972.

The Endangered Species Act of 1973

The Endangered Species Act of 1973 requires that the government protect all animal and plant life threatened with extinction. An **endangered species** is any plant or animal species whose ability to survive and reproduce has been jeopardized by human activities. A **threatened species** is one that is likely to become endangered. The Endangered Species Act requires the conservation of the ecosystems that support threatened or endangered species. Marine species are administered by the National Marine Fisheries Service (NMFS); the Fish and Wildlife Service (FWS) over-sees terrestrial, freshwater, and migratory bird species. Species are listed after intense study and public comment. The Act charges that the decision to include a species should be made solely on biological and not economic grounds. One provision is that federal agencies must consult with the NMFS and the FWS on any activity involving endangered species or their habitats. Additionally, no one is allowed to take or harass any endangered species. Once a species is listed, the goal is for it to recover and be removed from the list. The Act provides recovery guidelines.

be endangered. But if the species has low reproductive rates, or if the pollutant affects so many individuals that the population is seriously reduced, there may be long-term population effects. Also, damage to a population may be greater if the species is suffering stress from other sources, such as temperature increases. Pollution can be directly hazardous to human health. It can also impair fishing and hinder other marine activities.

WRAP-UP

Whether they enter the ocean by raining out of the atmosphere, by running off the land in streams and rivers, or by coming directly from industrial or municipal sources, large amounts of the pollutants generated by modern society end up in the sea. Once in the ocean, they often remain, although they may be diluted, dispersed, or broken down. Pollutants may also bioaccumulate in marine organisms so that animals at the top of the food web contain a much higher concentration of toxic substances than those at the bottom. Because humans often eat the large, predatory fish that make up the top level of the marine food web, people are also vulnerable to ingesting bioaccumulated pollutants. There are many categories of pollutants, which will be discussed in the following two chapters.

Nonbiological
Pollution

Large oil spills receive the attention of the press, politicians, and ordinary citizens, many of whom volunteer to help with the cleanup. Yet much more oil enters the sea from small oil spills each year. Other pollutants, some toxic, are constantly being added to the oceans. Pollutants can poison organisms, alter the development of their sex organs, or cause them to choke or drown. Plastic waste is ingested by marine organisms that mistake it for food, and abandoned fishing nets can drift through the seas catching marine life long after the nets have been abandoned by fishers. Pollutants can also change the acidity of the water so that shells and other structures dissolve or cannot form. Many pollutants are most concentrated where they enter the sea, and their concentration diffuses the farther they go from land.

OIL

Oil, particularly in large, deadly spills, is the marine pollutant that gets the most attention because oil can cause an enormous amount of damage to wildlife and the environment. Since it floats on water, ocean processes spread spilled oil rapidly over the sea surface. To combat a spill, the oil is first contained and then removed by skimmers or absorbents, a process that usually recovers only about 10% to 15% of the substance. Next, chemicals are applied to encourage some of the oil to disperse. Booms placed in the water keep the oil from reaching critical sites, such as seabird colonies or fish farms. Oil that reaches the shore may be removed by flushing or high-pressure washing with water, but this has proven to be damaging to wildlife. A safer procedure is to absorb the oil with straw or cut vegetation and then dispose

The *Exxon Valdez* Oil Spill

The largest oil spill in the United States was in 1989 when the *Exxon Valdez* oil tanker struck submerged rocks in Prince William Sound near Valdez, Alaska. The tanker's captain had downed 14 shots of vodka earlier that afternoon. After his ship left port, he put a helmsman in charge and retired to his quarters. A jury later found both Exxon and the captain negligent.

Within six hours of the collision, the tanker lost about 10.9 million gallons (40 million liters) of oil. No one with knowledge of spills was in the area during the crucial first three days when seas were calm. By the time a crew arrived, a storm had blown the oil onto the shoreline. Eventually, more than 10,000 people using containment booms, skimmer ships, bottom scrapers, and absorbent sheets arrived, but they were able to contain only 17% of the lost oil.

Natural cleansing processes were not effective since the oil was released into protected water instead of the open ocean. The oil coated more than 1,100 miles (1,700 km) of shoreline. Some estuaries had oil 3.3 feet (1 m) deep in places. An estimated 250,000 seabirds, including 900 bald eagles, perished; 2,800 sea otters, 300 harbor seals, 23 whales, and untold numbers of fish also died. The spill wrecked the sound's $150 million per year salmon, herring, and shrimp industry.

The *Exxon Valdez* disaster is the most studied oil spill in history, and most experts conclude that drastic steps should have been taken early on. As Gail Phillips, the executive director of the *Exxon Valdez* Oil Spill Trustee Council in Anchorage told *National Geographic News* in March 2004, "I was very upset at the time that we did not have the courage . . . to burn the ship. For the money that's been spent and the losses that are out there, it would have been cheap just to burn the ship."

of it. Over the days, weeks, and months that follow a spill, the oil in the water and on the land will be dispersed by currents and waves, broken down by sunlight, and biodegraded by bacteria.

The effect of an oil spill on marine organisms depends on the amount and type of oil, the weather and sea conditions, and the ecosystems the oil contacts. Refined oil is more toxic and has more damaging and longer-lasting effects than crude oil. Polynuclear aromatic hydrocarbons (PAHs), compounds found in weathered crude or refined oil, can be toxic to organisms even in very small doses.

An important lesson learned from the spill was that cleanup can cause more damage than the oil itself. Hot water (150°F, 65°C) that was used to blast oil from between rocks cooked small plants and animals or smothered them as the force of the water stirred up sand and rocks. Several years later, the cleaned areas were in worse shape than those that had been left alone.

Prince William Sound is nearly back to normal: Commercial fisheries are doing well and wildlife is abundant. But substantial subsurface oil lies beneath cobble beaches and is still toxic. Water cannot penetrate the oil, so nothing can live below it. Some animal populations seem not to have recovered, including common loons, harbor seals, harbor ducks, and Pacific herring. Sea otters get oil on their fur as they try to dig up clams, and their bodies contain elevated levels of petroleum byproducts.

Oily Guillemot on oil-covered rocks from the *Exxon Valdez* oil spill, Alaska. (© *John S. Lough/Visuals Unlimited*)

The effects of an oil spill evolve with time. For the first day or two after a spill, the hydrocarbons evaporate off the oil and kill some nearby aquatic organisms, particularly larvae and other young. For the next days and weeks, oil floating at the sea surface reduces the sunlight available for photosynthesis, causing primary productivity to decrease. Oil-sensitive red and green algae are often killed. Floating globs of oil coat seabird feathers and mammal fur, possibly causing the animals to lose their buoyancy and insulation. Many of them drown or die of exposure. When birds preen their oiled feathers, they ingest toxic compounds. Oil globs clog fish gills and kill larvae. Some oil sinks and smothers benthic organisms.

The long-term effects of oil spills are less well known. Rocky beaches that are frequently washed by storms may recover in one to two years, but quiet or enclosed beaches may take more than 10 years. Oil that penetrates down into sandy beaches may remain there indefinitely. Researchers have found a layer of contaminated sediment from a spill that took place more than 30 years ago near Woods Hole, Massachusetts. Plants and invertebrates that produce high numbers of young often recover quickly because there are lots of opportunities for the offspring to find more suitable places to live. Individual birds and mammals are lost to the spill, but others migrate into the area once it is clean, and typically the population recovers within a few years. Some ecosystems or organisms may take several decades to recover. With mangroves, for example, oil smothers their roots and the chemicals that enter the sediments may be toxic to the plants. PAHs reduce spawning success in some fish and are linked to genetic damage, malformations, and reduced growth and mobility in others.

Oil spills bring losses to humans as well as ecosystems. Spills damage coastlines that are valued for swimming, surfing, sportfishing, and other recreational activities. Seawater-using industries, such as power plants, may be disrupted, as are port and harbor operations. Damaged commercial fishing boats and fishing gear cost fishers money and strongly affect the catch. Fisheries recover fairly quickly from spills due to the high reproduction rate of most fish, but the taste of the fish is tainted by the flavor of oil.

After a disaster such as an oil spill, it is natural for people to want to mitigate the damage. One success story occurred in 2000, when a ship containing 1,300 tons of oil sank 20 miles (30 km) from Cape Town, South Africa. Amazingly, 90% of the 20,000 African penguins that were covered with oil survived due to the efforts of international teams working around the clock for six weeks. Penguins are relatively easy to save because they have fat to help them survive as they wait to be cleaned.

The *Exxon Valdez* disaster brought about regulations requiring that tankers be more environmentally sound. Single-hulled tankers are to be replaced internationally by double-hulled tankers by 2015 so that if the outer layer of the ship is punctured, there is another layer of steel for protection. Ship design and construction materials are also seeing improvements. Oil pipelines, particularly those that are aging, are in need of regulation as well. In some regions, such as the town of Valdez, Alaska, ships are escorted by tugboats until they reach open water. Vulnerable regions have more detailed emergency plans.

Major oil spills are certainly disasters, but about 10 times more oil enters the oceans from chronic, smaller-scale sources. These include discharge from normal ship operations, such as flushing ballast water; spillage and waste from oil drilling and production platforms; leaks from the outboard motors of small boats and Jet Skis (which release up to 30% of their fuel directly into the water); jettisoned aircraft fuel; and pollutants that rain out of the atmosphere. By far, the largest source of oil in the oceans is the day-to-day runoff from roadways and other land surfaces. About 16 million gallons (61 million l) of oil are carried by rivers and streams into North American coastal waters each year. Oil and other pollutants also enter the oceans when they are dumped illegally.

The effects of these small additions of oil are less well known than the effects of major spills. One reason is that oil in these small spills is often accompanied by other toxic chemicals. Being stressed by oil exposure makes animals more vulnerable to other problems, and that is what actually kills them or reduces their reproductive success.

Estimates are that hundreds of thousands of birds are killed by small oil slicks each year.

Diffuse sources of oil and other toxic chemicals, such as urban run-off, are not regulated or even monitored in most places. Communities should try to reduce the amount of land that is covered by impervious surfaces, such as parking lots, and increase the amount that is covered by such things as gardens to absorb runoff. Streams should be monitored for total hydrocarbons as well as PAHs, but tightening budgets have decreased the number of monitoring stations. Coastal development has increased pressure on sewage treatment plants; these plants should be upgraded so that storm water overflow is treated rather than dumped directly into streams and the ocean.

To reduce oil pollution in the seas, people must be educated to not dump oil or toxic materials into pipes that drain directly into a water body. More efficient motors should be developed for recreational watercraft. Developed nations should share environmentally sound technologies with developing ones, and industries should comply with environmental regulations in all countries, whether required to do so or not. Consumers should be willing to pick up the extra costs that are incurred by environmentally sound practices.

PERSISTENT ORGANIC POLLUTANTS

The man-made organic compounds that are used in pesticides, flame retardants, industrial solvents, and cleaning fluids are common and hazardous marine pollutants. Persistent Organic Pollutants (POPs) are synthetic organic chemicals that persist in the environment (meaning they do not biodegrade or dissipate) and bioaccumulate in the food web. Many are toxic, some even in small amounts. (A table of the "Dirty Dozen," the 12 POPs that are of most concern to the global community, is shown on page 99.)

POPs volatilize and enter the atmosphere, where they can travel thousands of miles from their nearest use. The chemicals can enter the sea from the atmosphere in rain, attached to dust particles, or

Persistent Organic Pollutants: The EPA's "Dirty Dozen"

CHEMICAL	TYPE
aldrin	pesticide
chlordane	pesticide
DDT	pesticide
dieldrin	pesticide
endrin	pesticide
heptachlor	pesticide
hexachlorobenzene	pesticide, industrial chemical, byproduct
mirex	pesticide
toxaphene	pesticide
polychlorinated biphenyls (PCBs)	industrial chemical, byproduct
dioxins	byproduct
furans	byproduct

they can be blown in on the wind. Rivers may bring small amounts of chemicals into the sea, which can be locally damaging, particularly during floods. Even compounds that have not been used for decades are concentrated near the mouths of major rivers due to illegal use and drainage from contaminated lands or unsafe disposal sites.

POPs are found throughout the oceans. Most POPs are insoluble in water but soluble in fats. The chemicals accumulate in the fatty acid film that floats at the sea surface and may be hazardous for birds, such as petrels, that skim the fat. POPs adsorb onto (adhere to the surface of) plankton to become part of the meal the plankton make for other organisms. "The ocean acts like a giant conveyor belt, carrying pollutants around the globe to the ocean-of-fat that consists of all the fat cells of ocean plants and animals," said Roger Payne of the Ocean Alliance in *Chemistry and Industry* magazine in March, 2005. Dust particles and shells with adsorbed compounds settle in the water column and are eaten by filter or bottom feeders.

The use of several of the most toxic pesticides has been phased out, but their damage persists. **DDT** was first used as a pesticide in 1939. The chemical was cheap; persistent in the environment; extremely toxic to insects, but less so to other animals; and seemingly safe for humans. After World War II, DDT was used to prevent typhus in Europe, to control malaria and other insect-borne disease in tropical areas, and to reduce pests in developed nations. But over time, it was found that DDT breaks down into extremely harmful compounds that accumulate in female birds, causing them to lay eggs with extremely thin shells. This process decimated the reproductive success of some bird species, particularly the fish-catching seabirds like pelicans, osprey, and the American bald eagle.

Marine mammals also bioaccumulate POPs. Although DDT has been banned in the United States since 1973, every sample of sperm whale skin and blubber taken today is contaminated with DDT compounds. Toxaphene, a relative of DDT, is still in use as a pesticide in the United States. The chemical is extremely toxic to fish and bioaccumulates in marine organisms.

Unlike other POPs, **polychlorinated biphenyls (PCBs)** are water soluble. These extremely stable compounds were once used as flame retardants; to cool and insulate electrical devices; to manufacture paints, plastics, adhesives, and other materials; and to strengthen wood and concrete. Although PCBs have been banned in industrialized nations for decades, they are everywhere in the environment, particularly in the animals at the top of the food web. Some Arctic polar bears have PCB levels as high as 80 ppm. Dolphins in United States coastal waters have PCB concentrations that are more than 100 times the amount defined by the United States government as safe.

PCBs interfere with reproduction, development, and other processes in birds and mammals. PCBs are thought to be responsible for behavior changes and declining fertility in seals and sea lions off California and for the weakened immune systems in Mediterranean dolphins. The chemicals interfere with the **metabolism** of thyroid hormones, the chemical messengers that regulate physiological processes, such as brain development and metabolism. In humans, exposure to high concentrations of PCBs has been linked to skin and respiratory problems; as yet, smaller amounts have not been shown to have an effect.

One of the most toxic chemicals known, **dioxin**, is not manufactured or used; it is an unwanted byproduct of the production of herbicides, disinfectants, and other chemicals. Dioxin also forms when some chemicals are burned, such as the plastic polyvinyl chloride. None of the 75 forms of dioxin serve any useful purpose, but they are ubiquitous in the environment. No living creature, no matter how remote its home, is completely untainted by the compound. Although the chemical's harmful effects are not yet fully understood, it may restrict an organism's ability to manufacture proteins and decrease immune system function. Some studies suggest that dioxin causes cancer and other serious illnesses. In laboratory experiments, moderate doses can cause spontaneous abortions in rats and developmental abnormalities, such as cleft palate, in mice. The effects of high doses on human health have been inconclusive.

Because POPs behave similarly, many have comparable environmental effects. In laboratory experiments, both DDT and PCBs reduce primary productivity in phytoplankton and may harm some marine fish, even those low on the food chain. Since POPs are stored in fats, they are most likely to become a problem during lean times, when animals metabolize their fat reserves and whatever chemicals are contained in them. In mammals, POPs are passed from mother to offspring, during pregnancy and in breast milk. Some human breast milk is so contaminated with some POPs that if it were cow's milk it would have been banned. Some environmentalists suggest that since these chemicals accumulate, seafood may someday become unfit to eat.

Since 2001, POPs have been regulated under the Convention on Persistent Organic Pollutants. Signatory nations have agreed to reduce or eliminate production or release of the "Dirty Dozen" and to work to determine which POPs will be added to the list in the future.

ENDOCRINE DISRUPTORS

Endocrine disruptors interrupt the functions of the endocrine system, the system that controls the body's internal environment by sending out hormones as chemical messengers. Most endocrine disruptors are estrogens or estrogen mimics. **Estrogens** are vertebrate female sex hormones that trigger the development of the sex organs and control the reproductive cycle. In concentrations that are too low to be toxic, these compounds act on the endocrine system, affecting endocrine function and reproduction. Endocrine disruptors include many POPs, such as DDT and PCBs, and other compounds, such as tributyltin (TBT), a substance described on page 104.

Sewage effluent contains high concentrations of synthetic estrogens, primarily from birth control pills and estrogen replacement therapies (which are sometimes used after menopause), both of which are among the most prescribed pharmaceuticals in the United States. These chemicals are not altered or stopped by sewage treatment facilities; they do not adsorb onto sediments, and they are not biodegradable. Endocrine disruptors are environmentally persistent and many bioaccumulate.

The highest concentrations of endocrine disruptors in the marine environment are found along coasts where there is the most sewage effluent. Concentrations in the open ocean are low or nondetectable. Male zooplankton with female reproductive parts have been found in coastal waters near sewage effluent. In experiments on marine invertebrates, such as sponges, crustaceans, mollusks, and echinoderms, environmental estrogens stimulate the development of ovaries or eggs, prevent the development of embryos, or cause cell damage or death.

Male fish exposed to environmental endocrines may develop smaller testes, have reduced sperm production, develop ovaries and produce eggs, or develop as females. The numbers of males and females may be skewed, the animals may develop poorly, or the population may be reduced. In mammals, males exposed to estrogens do not develop correctly sexually, or their sexual and reproductive success is inhibited. In an extreme example, seven years after a spill of an insecticide related to DDT in Lake Apopka, Florida, male alligators had tiny penises, 90% did not produce testosterone, 75% of alligators' eggs did not hatch (normally, only 5% of eggs fail to hatch), and those that did hatch produced sexually abnormal offspring.

In marine mammals, northern minke whales have been found with abnormal testes and bowhead whales with reproductive dysfunction. The only true hermaphroditic cetacean ever found was a beluga whale that had two testicles and two ovaries. This animal lived in the St. Lawrence Estuary of Canada, where the toxic soup the beluga whales swim in (which includes much more than just endocrine disrupting chemicals) has resulted in them having among the highest cancer rates of any wild animals. Some of these whales are so contaminated that their dead bodies qualify as hazardous waste.

HEAVY METALS

Some heavy metals are pollutants in nearly any concentration and others are pollutants only when concentrations are high. Natural processes release heavy metals into the environment. For example, iron and aluminum in rocks become wind-blown dust. Mercury is released in volcanic eruptions and lead in hydrothermal vent fluids. Human activities discharge heavy metals from coal combustion, electric utilities, steel and iron manufacturing, fuel oils, fuel additives, and trash incineration.

Heavy metals enter the ocean from runoff from the land, fallout from the air, and dispersion from shipwrecks. Large storms bring more metals into the water since they cleanse areas that have remained isolated for a long time. Rivers transport heavy metals from mining regions, urban areas, human waste, landfills, and adsorbed onto sediments. Metallic antifouling paints used to keep organisms from growing on the submerged portions of boats and marine structures bring high concentrations of heavy metals into marinas. Heavy metals are most concentrated in coastal regions, where they are released.

Living organisms require trace amounts of some heavy metals for life processes. Hemoglobin, the oxygen-transporting molecule, utilizes iron; many enzymes contain zinc. Other necessary metals include copper, vanadium, and cobalt. But even the biologically useful heavy metals are toxic in large enough quantities. The heavy metals mercury, lead, and cadmium are not biologically useful and are toxic even in tiny quantities. Excess heavy metals bioaccumulate and so are especially dangerous to organisms that feed high on the food chain.

Mercury is probably the most harmful heavy metal. Mercury is emitted by the burning of coal, municipal, and medical wastes, and by the mining and refining of some metal ores. Mercury vapor enters the air, then cools, condensing into tiny droplets that can travel hundreds of miles before falling into terrestrial or marine sediments, where bacteria convert it to an organic form, usually **methyl mercury**. While mercury alone is not harmful, methyl mercury is extremely toxic.

Mercury is poisonous to red algae and to the larvae of some small invertebrates. Methyl mercury is easily absorbed through the skin, lungs, and gut. The chemical does not appear to be toxic to seabirds and marine mammals, but the compound bioaccumulates in top predators like tuna. Humans are very sensitive to methyl mercury; it can cause brain, liver, and kidney damage. Recognition of the dangers of mercury to human health resulted in a great decrease in global mercury production beginning in 1990.

Tributyltin (TBT) is an extremely effective antifouling agent. TBT kills many planktonic organisms, including mollusk larvae. At sublethal doses, TBT reduces the growth rate and size of some invertebrates. The compound is also an endocrine disruptor and has caused some female dog whelks (a type of mollusk) to grow penises. TBT has also been linked to declines in marine snail populations, and it suppresses immune system function in vertebrates. In humans, TBT causes neural, respiratory, and psychological disturbances, plus abdominal pain and vomiting, among other problems. TBT antifouling paints have been banned in North America and many other countries for use on small boats, but they are allowed on oceangoing vessels.

SOLID WASTE

All over the world, the oceans are awash in trash. Solid waste—or trash—enters the ocean from beachgoers, ships and fishing boats, shipwrecks, and improper dumping on land. The International Convention for the Prevention of Pollution from Ships bans the disposal of all waste other than food into the sea, but the ban is often disregarded.

Plastic is the worst problem. Plastic is everywhere, with about 250 billion pounds (110 billion kg) produced each year. The substance is virtually indestructible, taking about 400 years to decompose. When broken down by sunlight, it just becomes plastic pellets, the building blocks of plastic products. An estimated 6.5 million tons (589 million kg) per year are discarded by ships, most within 250 miles (400 km) of the shore.

A 1987 survey found 46,000 pieces of plastic floating on the sea surface in each square mile of ocean off the northeastern United States. An independent study of debris floating in the North Pacific gyre in the early 2000s, led by Captain Charles Moore of the Algalita Marine Research Foundation, found that there were six pounds (2.7 kg) of plastic for every pound (.5 kg) of zooplankton. In the shipping lanes between Iceland and Scotland, scientists demonstrated that there was three times more plastic in the water column in the 1990s than there had been in the 1960s. Plastics even wash ashore in such remote locations as the Northwestern Hawaiian Islands Coral Reef Ecosystem Reserve (which was designated as the Northwestern Hawaiian Islands National Monument in 2006).

Transparent organisms such as jellies have been photographed with colored plastic showing through their bodies. Some organisms, including large fish and sea turtles, confuse plastic bags for jellies and accidentally eat them. White plastic pellets are mistakenly eaten by fish, turtles, marine birds, and other marine organisms. Even plankton may ingest the tiniest plastic fragments. Microscopic plastic bits also wash ashore and mix with beach sediments where they are ingested by deposit feeders.

An estimated 100,000 marine mammals and more than one million seabirds die each year from plastic debris in the ocean, according to the Marine Conservation Society of the United Kingdom. Marine mammals and birds become entangled in plastic nets or are muzzled by six-pack rings. Birds such as the Laysan albatross have been found

Plastic Trash in an Ecosystem Reserve

Plastics wash ashore, tainting even remote beaches far from where they were used. Jean-Michel Cousteau, son of famous oceanographer Jacques Cousteau, saw endless trash while filming a documentary on a pristine coral reef ecosystem on Kure, 1,000 miles (1,600 km) northeast of Oahu, Hawaii, in the Northwestern Hawaiian Islands Coral Reef Ecosystem Reserve. "Global ocean currents carry the marine debris to the Northwestern Hawaiian Islands, which are like the picket fencing stopping sand and snowdrifts," Cousteau said in *National Geographic News* on July 28, 2003.

The debris traps the critically endangered Hawaiian monk seals (*Monachus schauinslandi*), threatens Hawaiian green sea turtles (*Chelonia mydas*), and kills Laysan and black-footed albatross (*Diomedea immutabilis* and *Diomedia nigripes*) chicks who gulp down plastic particles. "Some birds—particularly Laysan and black-footed albatross chicks—have been affected and are found dead with all the plastic material visible in their stomach while the rest of their body decomposes," reported Cousteau.

Perhaps most damaging are discarded fishing nets that become snagged on the islands' coral reefs, where they trap other debris, forming large bundles extending 30 to 50 feet (10 to 15 m) into the ocean. The nets, weighed down by the debris, rip the surface of the reef like a bulldozer, finally ending in a "graveyard" of nets, as described by Russell Brainard of NOAA Fisheries in Honolulu, Hawaii.

To salvage the reef without causing further damage, divers must cut the nets away strand by strand, a difficult and dangerous process. Since 1996, the National Oceanic and Atmospheric Administration (NOAA) has spearheaded a cleanup effort to remove plastic debris from the reefs of the Northwestern Hawaiian Islands. More than one million pounds (450,000 kg) has been collected, but the currents always bring in more. "Until we remove it [the trash] from the ocean and eliminate the source, this will be a continuing problem," Brainard said. "It's been illegal for 25 years to put plastic into the ocean and it is still going into the ocean by one way or another."

A sea lion with an injury around its neck caused by plastic debris. (© *David Wrobel/Visuals Unlimited*)

coughing up an enormous range of plastic objects that had collected in their stomachs. Albatross chicks sometimes die from the trash in their stomachs.

Abandoned drift nets made of translucent plastic are almost impossible for marine animals to see, and the plastics do not break down for years. These so-called ghostnets may be hundreds of yards long and tens of yards wide. Ghostnets drift at around 25 to 50 feet (7.6 to 15.2 m) deep and ultimately are drawn by currents into relatively small areas. Sea birds, sea turtles, seals and porpoises become fatally trapped in the nets. In 2005, a Russian submersible became ensnared in a discarded fishing net and could not move. The seven member crew spent days huddled in the cold and dark, 600 feet (180 m) below the surface, as a British ROV cut the sub free just hours before the compartment ran out of oxygen.

Plastic fragments absorb toxic chemicals, such as DDT and PCBs, concentrating them up to one million times above the amounts found in the water. The toxins then can be ingested by filter or deposit feeders, which are then eaten by fish and ultimately passed on to top consumers, such as marine mammals, birds, and humans.

SEWAGE

Human and animal waste—sewage—is the most voluminous of disposed materials to enter the oceans. About 95% of sewage is water; **sewage sludge** is what remains after the water is removed. Although much sewage sludge is biodegradable, it also includes litter, pathogens, toxic metals, and synthetic organic chemicals. Some of this waste washes up on beaches, contaminates shellfish beds, and cause outbreaks of illnesses in people who consume raw oysters and clams.

Industrialized nations have built extensive sewage treatment systems that remove solids, pathogens, and some chemicals. Pipelines or barges transport treated sewage and sewage sludge to designated dump sites. Still, the sewage systems of many large cities are now old and overextended, so untreated sewage fouls some developed nations' waters. Some pollutants, such as parasite eggs and synthetic organic chemicals, are not removed by the treatment regimen. Sewage treatment also does not remove nutrients, a major problem in the coastal regions of many developed nations.

For developing countries, the cost of treating sewage is too high. Their large cities release hundreds of millions of tons of raw sewage into the sea each year. Even the Mediterranean Sea receives 30 to 50 million tons of raw or partially treated sewage each year.

SEDIMENT

The runoff of clay, silt, and sand from the land into the oceans is a natural and necessary process. However, human activities have caused erosion to occur in excess in some locations. Land that has been logged or plowed, for example, erodes more readily than land covered with natural vegetation.

Sediments entering the ocean can do a great deal of damage. Sediments cloud the water and hinder photosynthesis, bury benthic plants and animals, and clog animals' filter-feeding apparatus or gills. Coral reef ecosystems are sometimes completely buried by sediments, which have killed 75% of the coral reefs in the Philippines and in the Caribbean Sea off of Costa Rica. Australia's Great Barrier Reef receives five to ten times as much sediment as it did before the arrival of Europeans. Sediments may also contain fertilizers, heavy metals, and toxic chemicals that are harmful to marine organisms. Although they cause the most damage near shore, sediments that clog waterways and ports may be moved farther offshore, which moves their contaminants into deeper water.

Stopping sediment pollution in the oceans is difficult because the sediments are washed in from land. Farmers must use practices that minimize soil erosion, such as no-till farming and constructing stream bank fencing. Logging must also be done to minimize soil erosion, such as by taking individual trees rather than clear-cutting.

CARBON DIOXIDE

Even a common, abundant atmospheric gas is a pollutant if it is present in the atmosphere or oceans in excess amounts. Carbon dioxide (CO_2) is a byproduct of fossil-fuel burning. Its concentration in the atmosphere increased from around 280 parts per million (ppm) before the Industrial Revolution to about 381 ppm in 2006. Excess atmospheric CO_2 and other heat-retaining gases, known as **greenhouse gases**, brings about increased global temperatures, or **global warming**.

About one-third of the total amount of CO_2 produced by the burning of fossil fuels, or about 28 billion tons (25 billion metric tons) annually, is absorbed by the oceans. This keeps the greenhouse gas out of the atmosphere and reduces global warming. The addition of CO_2 to seawater, however, creates carbonic acid (HCO_3), which lowers the pH of the surface ocean. This decreases the availability of carbonate (CO_3) for shell and coral building and corrodes existing shells and corals.

The average surface ocean pH decreased from 8.25 in 1751 to 8.14 in 2004 and is forecasted to decrease to near 7.85 in 2100, according to a study by Christopher Sabine and Richard Feely published in the journal *Science*. Since pH is a logarithmic scale, a difference of 0.11 means that the water is about 30% more acidic than it was 250 years ago. The projected surface ocean pH for 2100 is lower than at any time in the last 420,000 years. Although atmospheric CO_2 contents have been higher during that time period, CO_2 levels are currently rising so rapidly that there is not enough time for the CO_2 to mix into the deep ocean and dilute the gas.

The consequences of increased acidification of marine life are already being seen. Decreased carbonate slows the growth and reproductive rates of plankton, corals, and other invertebrates. Already there has been an expansion of the ocean layers that dissolve shells and corals. By the middle part of the twenty-first century, coral reefs may have gaps that weaken their structure and make them more susceptible to storm damage. Organisms that cannot adapt to the acidic conditions may die out.

WASTE HEAT

Many marine organisms are sensitive to water temperature; this means that they can be adversely affected by excess heat. The most common source of excess heat in the marine environment is electrical generating plants, which use seawater for cooling. When this water is returned to the sea, its temperature may have increased as much as 22°F (12°C) (for oil- or coal-fired power stations) and 27°F (15°C) (for nuclear plants). Although the waste heat is quickly dissipated into the cold seawater, nearby organisms become stressed. This is especially true in tropical regions, where an increase in summertime water temperatures can bring death to creatures that cannot escape. Off the coast of Florida, for example, sponges, mollusks, and crustaceans can tolerate a summertime temperature increase of only about 3.6°F (2°C) to 5.4°F (3°C).

WRAP-UP

Industrialized society has expanded the types of pollutants that are added to the sea. Human activities are adding oil, trash, toxic chemicals, heavy metals, and heat as never before. Many of these pollutants are not removed, and their effects in the sea will be realized over the coming decades. The rampant addition of pollutants to the oceans is an ongoing experiment with effects on marine organisms and humans that have not yet been realized.

Biological Pollution

Biological pollutants are living organisms that are present in unnatural quantities or in places where they do not belong. Excess nutrients—from fertilizers, detergents, and human and animal waste—are pollutants because they encourage the growth of unnaturally large populations of algae or seaweed, which can damage natural ecosystems. Pathogens are microbes that are part of the natural environment, but they can cause animals and people to sicken. Species of organisms that colonize regions where they are not native may alter ecosystems and act as pollutants in some contexts.

HARMFUL ALGAL BLOOMS

Nutrients ordinarily enter the marine environment in upwelling zones or from runoff from land. These nutrients feed algae, just as fertilizers on land encourage the growth of plants. Spring and summer rains that increase runoff may instigate intense algal blooms, covering tens to hundreds of square miles (km) of coastal waters. Although blooms are natural, their number and intensity has increased dramatically in the past few decades, due to recent escalations in nutrients from increases in sewage, agriculture, and aquaculture.

Most algal blooms are harmful because they are toxic. Sometimes toxic algal blooms are called red tides for the red color of the algae, although the blooms also can be white, yellow, or brown. Scientists also use the term **harmful algal bloom (HAB)**, since blooms are harmful because they are toxic.

Toxic blooms can harm or kill animals through direct exposure, or they can bioaccumulate up the food web to where they become poisonous when eaten. In 1986, a toxic bloom killed more than 22 million fish on the Texas Gulf coast over the span of two months. In 1987, 19 humpback whales that were later found to have eaten mackerel contaminated with toxic algae, died off of Cape Cod and

A harmful algal bloom known as a red tide on the Bountiful Islands, in the Gulf of Carpentaria, Queensland, Australia. (© Bill Bachman/ Photo Researchers, Inc.)

washed ashore. People eating fish and shellfish contaminated by toxic blooms become sick.

In 1995, more than 500,000 fish, many with red and black sores, died in Chesapeake Bay. People who came into contact with the water in the bay developed sores and eye irritation along with breathing difficulties, nausea, and deficiencies in learning and memory. The cause was found to be *Pfiesteria piscicida*, a dinoflagellate that damages fish skin with toxins then feeds from the material that comes from the sores. A 1997 *Pfiesteria* bloom caused massive fish die-offs along

Maryland's eastern shore, leading consumers to avoid all seafood from the region despite assurances that no toxins had been detected in seafood products. That single event cost at least $50 million in lost seafood sales and lost revenues for recreational boat charters. The *Pfiesteria* blooms were caused by the enormous increase in chicken and pig farming in North Carolina in the 1980s that brought 50,000 tons (45 million kg) of animal waste per day into the Neuse river system, which runs to Maryland's eastern shore.

Algae that are not toxic cause harm in other ways. Some of them have long, barbed spines that cause mucus to build up in a fish's respiratory system until it suffocates. Dense algae at the sea surface may block light from reaching seaweeds, resulting in less food and safety for some fish and shellfish. Endangered mammals may not be able to increase their population if their food source has been reduced.

HABs are estimated to cost the United States at least $50 million per year due to the deaths of wild and farmed fish, shellfish, vegetation, and coral reefs; the closing of fisheries; the cost of monitoring the blooms; the impact on tourism; and the cost of medical treatment for anyone exposed. The waters off New England had high toxicity levels during the years 2005 and 2006 after more than 30 years with no measurable toxicity; this incidence caused scientists to speculate that a period of more frequent red tides is emerging.

EUTROPHICATION

When the excess nutrients run out, the algae die and the HAB ends. The zooplankton and other animals that were feeding on the algae, and the seaweeds that were feeding on the excess nutrients die, too. All the dead tissue sinks to the bottom and triggers a population explosion for bottom-dwelling bacteria, which use up great amounts of oxygen. If surface waters mix with the bottom waters, the oxygen is replenished. But if the water column is stable and there is no vertical mixing—as is common in the summer, near river mouths where there are variations in oxygen content, or in semi-enclosed bays and lagoons—the oxygen is not replaced. Water with little or no oxygen is termed **hypoxic** and the depletion of oxygen by bacteria is known as **eutrophication**. Because the nutrients that cause hypoxia run off the land, eutrophication occurs at the mouths of almost all of the world's large rivers.

Without oxygen, fish and other animals cannot survive, so hypoxic waters become **dead zones**, regions that are hostile to most forms of life. Normal waters contain as much as 10 ppm oxygen. At 5 ppm, marine animals have difficulty breathing. Sharks abandon the region at about 3 ppm and most other fish at about 2 ppm. Organisms that are unable to evacuate, such as shellfish, crabs, shrimp and starfish, begin to die at about 1.5 ppm oxygen. In hypoxic zones, O_2 levels may be as low as 0.5 ppm. A large dead zone forms a wall in middle and deep water that life cannot get across. Surface waters are not affected since they mix with atmospheric oxygen.

Fishers must travel out of a dead zone to reach their catch. Sometimes the fishing is very good just outside the hypoxic waters because fish and shrimp flee to the edge, but this also indicates that the region is becoming less habitable and that the population may soon collapse. Species that are not affected by hypoxia, such as inedible comb jellies and stinging sea nettles, may take over the habitat.

The history of the Black Sea serves as a warning for other regions. During the 1970s and 1980s, heavy fertilizer use in Eastern Europe prompted algal blooms that blocked sunlight and kept seagrass from photosynthesizing. In about five years, the natural ecosystem was replaced by comb jellies, an invasive species from the Chesapeake Bay. (**Invasive species** are organisms that are introduced by human activities into a location where they are not native.) The comb jellies were so successful that in a few years their combined weight in the Black Sea exceeded the entire world's commercial fish catch. These jellies were later displaced by another invasive species of comb jelly from eastern North America. The Black Sea is now showing weak signs of recovering because the countries that drain into it can no longer afford fertilizer.

In the United States, dead zones occur in partially enclosed waters where there is nearby urban development. One of the largest and most persistent dead zones in United States waters is in the northern Gulf of Mexico.

The number of major dead zones around the world has been doubling roughly every decade since the 1960s. Between 1990 and 2006, the number nearly tripled to 2,000, according to the United Nations

The Gulf of Mexico Dead Zone

The Gulf of Mexico dead zone has been known by fishers for more than a century, but in the past two decades it has generally appeared earlier and become larger, although it varies each season. In the 1990s, the size of the dead zone doubled to about 7,000 square miles (18,000 square km). In 2002, it was more than 8,000 square miles (21,000 square km)—about the size of New Jersey. The growth of the zone is not surprising since triple the amount of fertilizer presently runs downstream compared to the flow during the period from the 1950s to the 1970s. More intense flood protection has also contributed. Whereas floodwaters once flowed over river banks and dumped nutrients into the ground, flood protection now keeps the nutrients in the river so they drain into the Gulf.

Eutrophication in the Gulf develops in spring and early summer. Normal oxygen contents in Gulf waters are about 6.3 ppm. About 7 to 10 days after spring rains begin in the agricultural regions, the oxygen content in the dead zone decreases to as low as 0.6 ppm, with the most intense hypoxia between 30 and 60 feet (9 to 18 meters) below the surface. The Mississippi River drains 41% of the land surface of the United States, including the rich Midwestern farmland. Spring rains grab excess fertilizers from the soil as well as excess nitrogen from animal manure, golf courses, urban lawns, and water-treatment plants. The Gulf dead zone disappears when autumn storms mix hypoxic bottom waters with oxygen-rich surface water.

The Gulf of Mexico provides 70% of the shrimp catch and two-thirds of oysters each year in the United States. The dead zone forces fishers to move farther from shore and may decrease the quality of their catch. The most commercially valuable species, brown shrimp, is 20% to 25% lighter in fat content when caught in low-oxygen waters. However, the Atlantic croaker, a bottom-dwelling finned fish, shows no difference in fat content.

Researchers recommend a 40% to 45% annual cutback in nitrogen use in the Mississippi River drainage area to decrease the Gulf dead zone to 3,000 square miles (5,000 square km). Nutrient runoff could be reduced if farmers planted crops that cover the ground year round rather than only part of the year. Since wetlands bacteria break down nutrients, farmers could

Environmental Programme. Eutrophication is a difficult problem to solve because the people and industries that are most affected by the problem are not those that cause the problem.

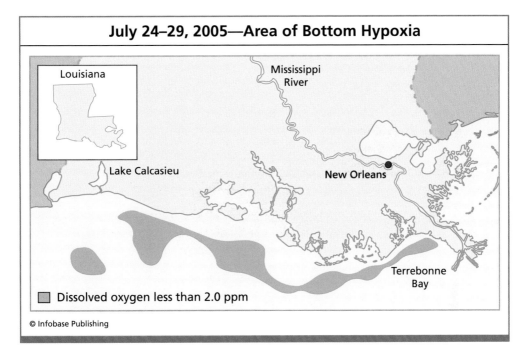

July 24–29, 2005—Area of Bottom Hypoxia

Louisiana

Mississippi River

Lake Calcasieu

New Orleans

Terrebonne Bay

☐ Dissolved oxygen less than 2.0 ppm

© Infobase Publishing

The Gulf of Mexico dead zone as surveyed on July 24–29, 2005. The shaded area depicts the portion of the gulf in which dissolved oxygen content is less than 2.0 ppm.

be encouraged to create marshes around their fields. By pumping polluted water through the wetlands, bacteria would convert the nitrates to nitrogen gas.

The history of the Gulf resembles that of the Black Sea, and no one knows how close the fishery is to collapsing. So far, only voluntary nutrient reduction measures have been called for, and many scientists think these measures are not enough to reduce the dead zone. Suggestions for a remedy include a federal cap on nitrate emissions for each state and regulation of even small sources of nitrates.

PATHOGENS

Pathogens are natural parts of any environment, but human activities may increase their distribution and amount. Sewage contains pathogens and parasite eggs, some of which survive a trip through the sewage treatment plant. A person can become infected through a cut or by swallowing contaminated seawater. Globally, swimming in contaminated water results in hundreds of millions of illnesses each year. Eating contaminated seafood is an enormous problem in some developing nations where precautions are not taken to ensure that seafood is clean; much of it is eaten raw.

Pathogens can affect other organisms, including marine mammals. Hundreds of sea otters have been found dead along the California coast each year since 2000, which is significant to a population of less than 3,000 animals. The causes of death are two parasites, both found in terrestrial animals: one in wild and domestic cats, and one in the opossum. The recent increase in otter deaths from parasites may be due in part to new flushable cat litters. The parasite eggs travel through the sewage treatment system and into the coastal waters, where they bioaccumulate in shellfish and are eaten by otters.

INVASIVE SPECIES

An entire ecosystem can be altered by the introduction of a new species. If the species was introduced by human activities, the new species can be considered a form of biological pollution. In most cases, the introduced organisms cannot survive in the new environment and they perish. If invasive species live with the natives, they add to the **biodiversity**—the number of different species—of the ecosystem. On rare occasions, the invasive species thrive; they have no predators and out-compete the native species for food and living space. Exploding populations of invasive organisms greatly decrease the diversity of an ecosystem by driving the natives toward extinction or by altering the habitat, so that it is no longer suitable for the native species. The rate of species invasion has risen exponentially over past 200 years.

Ships serve as the main carriers of invasive species to new marine ecosystems. Ballast water is taken onto an empty oil tanker to keep the ship stable on its return voyage to collect more oil. The ballast contains whatever local organisms were swimming in the water when it was taken on, such as plankton, jellies, sea stars, and larval mollusks and crustaceans. When the ballast water is dumped to allow the ship to take on oil, it includes the nonnative species, which may invade the new environment. Species can also be brought to new environments through canals, attached to boats and propellers, packed in bait worms, and through the aquaculture industry.

A group of sea squirts, genus name *Didemnum*, that invaded New England in the early 1990s is now found from Connecticut to Maine and in the Georges Bank fishery, where it coats about 90 square miles (230 square km) of the seafloor. With no predators, it spreads rapidly, smothering everything in its path including scallops and mussels, replacing native sea squirts, and making the area less hospitable to fish and shellfish larvae. No one knows if it came as ballast on cargo ships or on imported shellfish used in aquaculture. *Didemnum* has been found off the Pacific Northwest coast as well. According to Dann Blackwood of the U.S. Geological Survey (USGS) in Oceanus in 2005, "Nothing really wants to eat it. Nothing grows on it. And nothing seems to prevent it from spreading."

Tropical aquarium fish and plants can become invasive when dumped into warm waters, such as those in Florida. In a 2004 survey, 16 aquarium species were found in 32 spots there. The lead researcher, marine biologist Brice Semmens of the University of Washington in Seattle, told *National Geographic News* in 2004, "Releasing non-native reef fish is like playing Russian roulette with tropical marine ecosystems." A species of Caribbean seaweed used in aquariums has been spreading along the Mediterranean coastline off Spain, France, Italy, and Croatia since the 1980s; it is now costing millions of dollar each year to eradicate it in southern California bays.

The cost of dealing with invasive species in the United States is nearly $140 billion per year. Once a species establishes a foothold in the environment, it is difficult or impossible to stop. The best approach is to stop the invasion before it happens, yet it is difficult to figure out how to do this. Alan Burdick, author of *Out of Eden: An Odyssey of Ecological Invasion*, wrote, "Our current environmental legislation is poorly equipped to cope with this kind of invasion. Laws like the Endangered Species Act are intended to protect specific, known organisms from specific, known threats. Ecological invasion does not submit to such clarity."

The National Aquatic Invasive Species Act of 2005 was introduced to provide money for research, the monitoring and control of new and existing threats, and to regulate ballast water. The act followed earlier acts that responded to the zebra mussel invasion of the Great Lakes and other inland waters. These mollusks displace valuable native species and block water intake pipes, costing millions of dollars annually. Burdick says, "Critics may carp about the cost—$836 million over several years—but that is a small fraction of the cost that the zebra mussel already exacts."

Also, efforts are being made to introduce nonnative species into some environments to replace native species that are in decline. For example, due to pollution and parasites, the population of native oysters in the Chesapeake Bay is only one percent of what it was in prehistoric times. The bay water is less clean now than it was far in the past, when the entire volume of the bay was sieved by the filter-feeding shellfish once every three days. Efforts to bring back native oysters make little headway as long as the pollutants remain. As a result, seafood gatherers and processors are campaigning to introduce hardier Asian oysters to the bay to see if they can survive the parasites, filter the water, and be harvested for consumption. Experiments are in progress to determine whether the risks of introducing species are worth the benefits of having a thriving shellfish population.

WRAP-UP

Although biological pollutants are living organisms, they may be as hazardous to ecosystems as nonbiological pollutants. The introduction of excess nutrients into coastal waters generates HABs and eutrophication. To stop these serious problems it is necessary to reduce the runoff of excess nutrients into water bodies. Regulations must be put in place to stop the introduction of invasive species whose proliferation is costly and damaging to ecosystems.

Ozone Loss, Global Warming, and the Oceans

Some widespread and potentially irreversible environmental problems are the result of atmospheric pollution. In recent years, the ozone layer, which protects life on the Earth from the Sun's harmful **ultraviolet radiation (UV)**, has been under attack from manmade chemicals that break down the ozone, particularly in the spring in the skies over Antarctica. Ozone loss allows UV to penetrate the sea surface, damaging plankton and the Southern Ocean food web. Global warming is caused by the buildup of heat-trapping atmospheric gases, which are released primarily by the burning of fossil fuels and forests. Temperature increases affect marine life, particularly corals, which are extremely temperature sensitive. Global warming may also increase the number and intensity of El Niño events and change global ocean circulation patterns, which would alter the weather and climate of some locations.

OZONE LOSS AND THE OCEANS

The ozone layer of the Earth's upper atmosphere protects the planet and its life from the Sun's harmful ultraviolet radiation (UV). In the early

1970s, scientists performed calculations showing that some man-made compounds, including chlorofluorocarbons (CFCs), could travel into the upper atmosphere and break down the ozone. Ozone measurements found no evidence of this breakdown until the early 1980s when the **ozone hole** was discovered growing over Antarctica and the Southern Ocean each spring and early summer. The discovery of the ozone hole prompted the international community to band together to phase out ozone-destroying substances. Although the production of many of these substances has been substantially reduced, those ozone-destroying substances that have already been released will continue to destroy ozone for decades until they eventually break down in the upper atmosphere.

The Antarctic spring also brings about an enormous phytoplankton bloom that forms the base of the bountiful Southern Ocean food web. When ozone is depleted, harmful UV penetrates the water down to a depth of 66 feet (20 m). Since plankton are made of only one or a few cells, they cannot absorb radiation the way larger organisms with multiple layers of cells can, so UV causes serious damage to them. Although plankton may avoid high UV levels by sinking deeper into the water, this decreases the amount of visible light that is available to the organisms for photosynthesis.

During the period when the ozone hole is overhead, Antarctic phytoplankton produce up to 12% less food per day, equaling a 2% to 4% annual productivity loss. With less food, there is less energy available for the phytoplankton to reproduce. Fewer phytoplankton provide less food for zooplankton so their numbers are reduced, and so on up the food web. Animals that depend on Antarctic krill include 120 species of finfish, 80 species of seabirds, 6 species of seals, and 15 species of whales and dolphins. People also derive a great amount of food from the Southern Ocean food web. Experiments show that UV radiation may damage early developmental stages of fish and marine invertebrates.

GLOBAL WARMING AND THE OCEANS

Atmospheric greenhouse gases trap heat and cause the atmosphere to warm. Without this warming, Earth's average atmospheric temperature would be too low for complex life forms. But human activities, such as fossil fuel combustion and burning forests, are increasing atmospheric greenhouse gas levels and bringing about global temperature increases. In the century between 1900 and 2000, global temperature rose 1°F (0.6°C). Since the early 1970s, temperatures have risen more rapidly, with an increase of about 0.7°F (0.4°C), including a major upswing that occurred during the 1990s.

The effects of global warming are being seen around the world. Winters are shorter, glaciers and ice caps are melting, and the weather is becoming less predictable: Catastrophic floods, record-breaking heat waves, and unprecedented hurricane activity have all been attributed to global warming.

Nearly half the total CO_2 released by fossil-fuel burning in recent decades has been absorbed by the top layers of the seas. This has lessened increases in atmospheric CO_2 and the resultant temperature increases. While this is good for global temperatures, the added CO_2 has both chemical and biological impacts, such as increased seawater acidification, which is discussed in Chapter 9.

Meanwhile, greenhouse gases continue to be pumped into the atmosphere. Most climate models show that if no changes are made in greenhouse gas emissions, global average temperature will rise about 5°F (2.8°C) by around 2080. A greater temperature increase will occur at the poles; for example, as much as 12°F (6.7°C) at the North Pole. Rising temperatures will melt glaciers and polar ice caps, and the sea level will continue to rise. Coastal regions, where about one-third of the world's population lives and an enormous amount of economic infrastructure is concentrated, will flood. A 1-foot (30 cm) sea level rise in Florida would cause the loss of 100 feet (30 m) of beach. By 2080, rising seas could force hundreds of millions of people, particularly in nations without the resources to protect their coastlines, to abandon low-lying coastal areas. The rising sea level may destroy coral reefs, accelerate coastal erosion, and increase the amount of seawater that enters groundwater systems in coastal regions. Increasing temperatures will increase the frequency and intensity of storms, adding to the problems caused by the rising sea level.

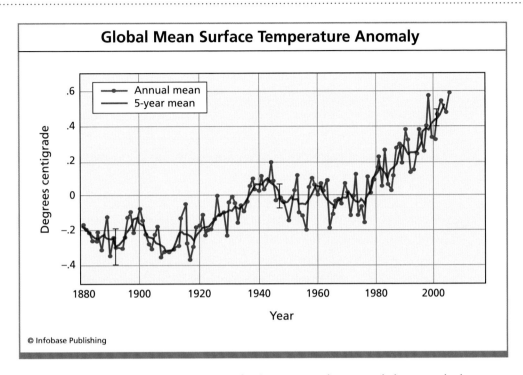

Global Mean Surface Temperature Anomaly

Global mean surface temperature anomaly since 1880, when records began to be kept. The zero line is the mean temperature from 1880 to the present. Global temperatures have been rising since 1880, but they have been increasing at a more rapid rate since the late 1970s.

Animal life is being adversely affected by global warming, a trend that will continue. According to a July 2005 *Seattle Times* article, a West Coast warming trend that began in 2002 resulted in coastal ocean temperatures 2°F to 5°F (1°C to 2.8°C) above normal in summer 2005. The trend continued in summer 2006. A change in wind patterns reduced upwelling, and the resulting loss of cold, nutrient-rich water resulted in the loss of phytoplankton and krill.

"In 50 years, this has never happened," said Bill Peterson, an oceanographer with the NOAA in Newport, Oregon. "If this continues, we will have a food chain that is basically impoverished from the very lowest levels."

The demise of plankton populations resulted in a large number of seabird deaths (between 5 and 10 times higher than normal for

Brandt's cormorants along the southern coast of Washington); fewer salmon (a 20% to 30% drop in juvenile salmon populations off the coasts of Oregon, Washington, and British Columbia); and other oddities, such as the appearance of warm-water plankton and jellyfish piling up on beaches. Some species of seabirds (for example, common murres and Cassin's auklets) began breeding late, and many abandoned their colonies without having bred successfully. Dead birds showed signs of starvation due to lack of plankton and other food sources. Food stress also makes the animals more vulnerable to other stresses. Warm years along the West Coast have also brought excess deaths of fur seals, sea lions, and gray whales.

Air temperatures over the Antarctic Peninsula have warmed by 4.5°F (2.5°C) over the past 50 years, about five times more than the global mean rate. Antarctic krill populations have dropped by about 80% since the 1970s in the Southern Ocean. This is likely due to the loss of sea ice as temperatures rise because the krill feed on algae found under the ice. The loss of sea ice as a feeding platform may also have led to the decline of several species of penguins.

Rising water temperatures increase the success of heat-tolerant nonnative species at the expense of some native species. The decline of krill in the Southern Oceans has led to an increase in the population of jellylike animals known as salps. The warmer temperatures will likely speed the metabolisms of some ectotherms, which may harm their ability to survive and reproduce. Coral polyps are extremely temperature sensitive, and coral reefs are expected to decline in abundance.

OCEAN CURRENTS AND CLIMATE CHANGE

Rising sea surface temperatures are expected to have an increasing effect on ocean circulation. Higher ocean temperatures in the western Pacific seem already to have increased the frequency and duration of El Niño events. In decades past, El Niño events came every five years and lasted up to 18 months; many were barely noticeable. Over the past 25 years, mean equatorial Pacific sea surface temperature has increased roughly 1.5°F (0.8°C), and El Niños have been taking place

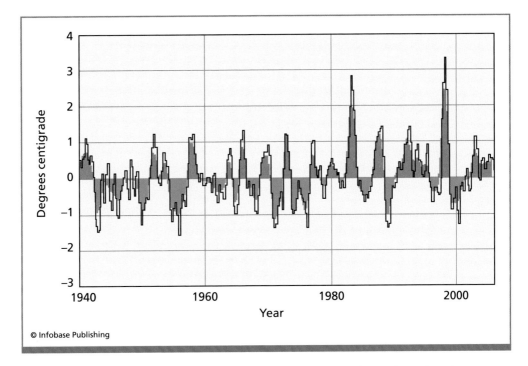

Sea surface temperature anomalies in the Pacific Basin from 4°N to 4°S and 150°W to 90°W. The outer line is the 5-month running mean; the shaded regions depict the 13-month running mean. Data since 1949 are measured; data before 1949 are reconstructed. High SST correlates with El Niño events; low SST correlates with La Niña events, although there is an overall trend to warmer SST temperatures visible.

roughly every three years, with durations so long that they sometimes nearly overlap. Greater increases in Pacific Ocean warming could bring about a nearly permanent El Niño, with the cool water events separated by decades. This situation would cause a long-term change in weather patterns.

Large ocean currents are stable in the long term, and they influence climate in many regions. Nowhere is that more obvious than with the Gulf Stream, which raises the air temperature of the British Isles and northwestern Europe by about 9°F (5°C). The Gulf Stream is pulled northward in part by the sinking of very dense North Atlantic water. If increased global temperatures cause a decrease in sea ice formation and bring about the melting of nearby glaciers in the North

Atlantic, surface water there may no longer be dense enough to sink. This would keep the Gulf Stream from being pulled northward, which would rapidly cool the British Isles and northern Europe.

If the Gulf Stream ceases to flow northward, the ocean and atmosphere in the region would be expected to cool by about 5.4°F to 12.6°F (3°C to 5°C), which is comparable to the Little Ice Age of the sixteenth to eighteenth centuries. While no one is certain that this will occur, the salinity of the North Atlantic has been decreasing for the past few decades, and North Atlantic bottom currents have experienced a 20% decrease in flow since 1950. Although similar measurements for the Gulf Stream have not been collected, that current is likely to have slowed also.

If North Atlantic water no longer sank, gases and nutrients would no longer make their way into the deep sea, and deep ocean life would suffer. Even scarier is the possibility that a warming of deep ocean water would melt the methane hydrates found on the continental margins. This would release the methane and increase its concentration in the atmosphere. Because methane is a powerful greenhouse gas, this could result in a scenario in which average global temperature rises so much and so quickly that nothing can stop it.

Reducing global warming will be much more difficult than stopping ozone depletion. Decreasing or eliminating the addition of greenhouse gases to the atmosphere necessitates converting to other energy sources, such as solar, tidal, and perhaps even nuclear power. Progress in this area requires a reduction in energy use and the development of technologies to reduce the formation of greenhouse gases or sequester the gases once they are formed. Cutting greenhouse gases requires a commitment from developed nations to reduce fossil fuel consumption and a commitment from developing nations to learn to rely on technologies that are not so environmentally destructive.

WRAP-UP

The past decade has seen nearly all scientists come around to the idea that the globe is warming and human activities are the primary cause. To avoid dangerous climate change, all the nations of the world must participate in reducing greenhouse gas emissions. Emissions caps must be instituted, alternative energy sources must be found and widely adopted, and technologies to remove greenhouse gases from the atmosphere must be developed. Meanwhile, temperatures will continue to rise and people must prepare to adapt for the changes that are already inevitable.

PART FOUR

HUMAN EFFECTS ON OCEAN ORGANISMS AND HABITATS

Overfishing

For millennia, the oceans supplied fish and seafood to fishers who fished from shore or small boats to feed their families and communities. Because fish produce many offspring, their populations remained high. The advent of industrialized fishing, the explosion of human populations, and the expectation that seafood should be widely available have rapidly increased the demand on fisheries, with **overfishing** being the result. A fishery is overfished when there are not enough mature animals to breed and replenish the species. Nowadays, fishing techniques are more destructive than they once were, and many more boats are harvesting from each active fishery. Until recently, when one fishery was overexploited, a new fishery usually was discovered. But now there are few or no new fisheries to be found, and management practices that work toward the long-term sustainability of a fishery must be put into place.

FISHERIES AND OVERFISHING

When a fishery is first discovered, the catch per unit effort (weight of fish caught versus vessel days of fishing) is high. Fish are plentiful and the season is lucrative. This attracts the attention of other fishers, which may initially increase the total catch. However, when the advanced fishing boats and factory ships move in, the fishery begins to suffer. Eventually, although the expenditure of effort and money increases, the fish catch decreases.

Overfishing occurs when the catch per unit effort and the total catch both decline. Often the fish are harvested before they are old enough to reproduce or before they have spawned enough times. In some species, older females produce more (and healthier) eggs and larvae. Thus, capturing too many young fish is detrimental to the fishery. Ultimately, the fishery becomes commercially dead, meaning that it is no longer economically feasible.

In its 2006 biennial report, "The State of World Fisheries and Aquaculture (SOFIA)," the UN Food and Agricultural Organization (FAO) estimated that two-thirds of fish stocks on the high seas are overfished, while most stocks close to shore are failing or are being fished to the maximum. In all, 25% of stocks are overexploited, and 52% are fully exploited. The catch has been stationary at between 85 and 95 million tons since the late 1980s. The U.S. Office of Fisheries Conservation and Management says that 41% of species in U.S. waters are overfished.

The situation for individual species is no better. Seven of the top 10 marine fish species are fully or overexploited; harvesting increases would have serious consequences to their populations. Large fish populations have been decimated to the point that only 10% of tuna, marlin, swordfish, sharks, cod and halibut remain compared to the populations of the 1950s. A *Science* magazine report in November 2006 projected that populations of all species of wild seafood will collapse before 2050 if fishing practices are not drastically altered. Yet, according to the United States National Marine Fisheries Service, global seafood demands will more than triple from 2004 to 2025.

HARMFUL FISHING PRACTICES

Modern fishing techniques are so effective at catching fish that they do a great deal of damage to marine life and to the environment. Long-line fishing catches everything that is attracted to the bait. Gill nets, too, are indiscriminate since they are transparent and cannot be seen by marine life. Perhaps worst are bottom trawlers, which scrape the seafloor of most of its life. Amazingly, several world governments including Japan, South Korea, Spain, Australia, and Russia, pay large subsidies, totaling over 150 million per year, to the bottom trawler fleet so that the fishers do not lose money.

Animals that are caught or killed in the process of fishing for other species are called **bycatch**. The U.N. estimates that about 25% of all fish caught are bycatch. Shrimp trawlers capture the most bycatch, between 2 and 10 pounds (1 and 4.5 kg) of sea life for every one pound of shrimp. Unwanted animals include fish that are too small, too low in value, or that the fisher is not licensed to catch. Birds and mammals also become caught in the fishing gear and drown. All seven species of marine turtle are endangered because each year about 12,000 die as bycatch.

Destructive fishing techniques are not the only problem facing fisheries. Each year, simply too many fish are caught. In his 2003 book, *Heal the Ocean*, scientist and environmentalist Rod Fujita outlines several problems with the way fisheries are managed. The most important, according to Fujita, is that too many boats are chasing too few fish. According to the World Wildlife Fund, there are about twice as many fishing boats as can fish sustainably. Although the market economy is supposed to work to reduce the number of fishing boats when the catch becomes too small to support them, governments reduce the effects of market forces by providing money for buying boats when catch numbers are down. Worldwide fishing subsidies total about $13 billion per year.

Fujita also decries "open access" fisheries. Most fisheries allow anyone equipped with a boat to hunt for animals. There is no incentive for a fisher to leave a fish behind to spawn because it will likely be taken by the next fisher. In this system, conservation is not rewarded.

FISHERIES IN TROUBLE

Fisheries around the world are in various stages of overexploitation. The once extraordinary North Atlantic cod fishery on the Georges Banks, which is located off the coasts of the United States and Canada, is a distressing example of fishery collapse. Cod are ground fish that feed on small fish, crabs, squid, and clams. The fish live 20 to 25 years and become sexually mature in 3 to 7 years. Since each spawning fish produces several million eggs, cod fisheries were once able to sustain heavy fishing.

Fishers fished cod with hand lines for nearly 400 years. One story goes that the fish were so dense in the water that fishers could walk from ship to shore on their backs. At the end of the nineteenth century, the Georges Banks fishery produced catches of 50,000 tons (45 million kg) a year. Around that time, fishing with longlines and trawl nets began, and in the 1950s huge European factory trawlers joined the hunt. The fishery peaked in 1968, with a catch of 810,000 tons (730 million kg). In the 1970s, even with intensified fishing efforts, the catch decreased to 200,000 tons (18 million kg).

The decline in the catch prompted Canada and the United States to exclude foreign vessels from their waters and introduce **quotas** that set limits to the amount of fish that can be harvested from a fishery in a season. Initially, the quotas were ignored and fishing efforts increased. In 1992, a temporary moratorium was placed on the Newfoundland cod fishery; large parts of the United States cod fishery were closed in 1993. Tens of thousands of people in both Canada and the United States lost their jobs. In 1994, only 2,700 tons (2.4 million kg) of cod were caught. By 2000, the population of mature fish was estimated at 97% below 1990 levels, which were already very low. Fishers desperate to earn a living endangered their lives by fishing farther from shore and in bad weather. In 2003, the rest of the fishery was closed. Some scientists say that a full moratorium will bring the population back to the healthy levels of the 1950s and 1960s, but others are not sure because bottom trawlers destroy the seafloor habitat that the young fish need to survive.

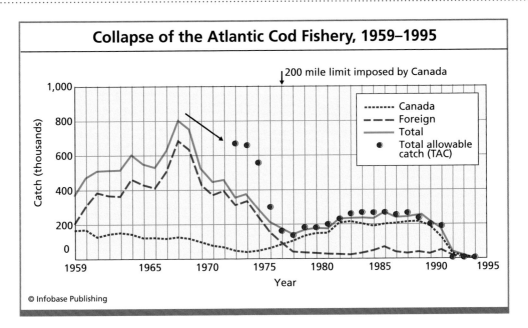

Collapse of the Atlantic Cod Fishery, 1959–1995

© Infobase Publishing

Between 1967 and 1977, total catches of North Atlantic cod declined dramatically due to overfishing. TAC values represent the catch fisheries managers would have allowed during those years.

Overfishing has brought other fisheries to the edge of collapse. The Patagonian Toothfish, which swims near Antarctica, is important to the diets of sperm whales and elephant seals. Marketed more appetizingly as the Chilean sea bass, the fish was one of the species that replaced the North Atlantic cod on people's dinner tables. Like other deepwater fish, these predators are slow to mature, breeding at 10 to 12 years old and living until they are at least 45 years old. A fully grown fish is over 6.5 feet (2 m) long and 220 pounds (100 kg). The Patagonian Toothfish was harvested by trawling beginning in the mid-1970s. A large stock was discovered in 1985, and a longline fishery developed rapidly. Reduced population numbers have stimulated illegal, as well as legal, fishing activity, and a single animal now can be priced as high as $1,000. In the mid-to-late 1990s, the illegal catch was two to three times that of the legal catch. Although the fishery is now better monitored, certain stocks have already collapsed, and poaching remains a problem. Without better regulation, the entire fishery may collapse in a few years.

Although humans do not eat krill, this fishery may also be in danger. The animals are attracting increasing amounts of attention from aquaculturists, who need enormous supplies of fish oil and fish meal for fish farming. The biotechnology industry is interested in krill because they contain substances that may be beneficial for treating heart disease, premenstrual tension, and skin cancer. Although the fishery is just beginning to be overused, it is now under the protection of the Commission for the Conservation of Antarctic Marine Living Resources (CCAMLR). The commission represents over 20 nations and is charged with balancing commercial fishing interests with conservation in the seas around Antarctica.

WHEN A FISHERY IS LOST

When a fishery is seriously reduced or collapses, the entire ecosystem is affected. In some cases, the loss of a species allows other organisms to flourish. The overfishing of trigger fish in Kenya allowed the population of sea urchins, their preferred food, to explode, causing damage to coral reefs.

The loss of a species may also cause a decline in the population of other organisms. An anchovy fishery once supported about 20 million seabirds on the famous "Bird Islands of Peru." In the 1950s and 1960s, about 85% of the anchovies were captured. An El Niño caused the fishery to collapse in 1972. By the late twentieth century, the seabird population had dropped to only five million birds, and today many of the islands have almost no birds. Similarly, the halving of the Alaskan pollock population may have led to a drop of 94% in Steller sea lion populations in some regions.

People also suffer when a fishery is lost. In the United States, the seafood industry provides 250,000 jobs and adds $30 billion annually to the nation's economy. Fishery collapse may plunge entire regions into recession and economic instability, as happened when the North Atlantic cod fishery collapsed. In developing nations, fishery collapse undermines food security and decreases the money available for economic development.

Up until now, the collapse of one fishery has led to the exploitation of another. Even fish that were not considered valuable before are at risk. As more desirable fish have become scarce, the Alaskan pollock, a tasteless bottom fish, has been processed and flavored to be sold as artificial crab, shrimp, and scallops, with the result that the pollock is now being overfished. This shift of fishing resources to a different species in order to replace a declining species cannot continue since there are few under-exploited fisheries left.

PROTECTING AND REBUILDING FISHERIES

For commercial fishing to continue as a viable industry, healthy fisheries must be protected, and decimated fisheries must be rebuilt. The 1996 Sustainable Fisheries Act, also called the Magnuson-Stevens Fishery Conservation and Management Act, attempts to guide fisheries in the United States' Exclusive Economic Zone (EEZ) toward sustainability. The act oversees management and monitoring of fisheries and promotes protection of essential fish habitat. While this act has assisted with the ongoing recovery of many species (Atlantic black sea bass, scup, summer flounder, sea scallops, yellowtail flounder, and king mackerel), the act is under attack from fishing organizations that say it is too rigid. The steps laid out by the act for protecting and rebuilding fisheries are discussed in the following paragraphs.

Research

The first step to protecting a healthy fishery is to understand the life cycles of the fish and their dependence on their environment. Research might have saved the now-closed white abalone fishery off California. Because white abalone produce enormous quantities of eggs, fisheries managers thought the animals could sustain a large harvest. But, as was later discovered, white abalone must live within a dense population of other abalone in order to breed successfully. Abalone hunters had been allowed to take the animals from wherever they found them, but the remaining populations were spread so thinly that they were unable to reproduce successfully. Fishing of white abalone might still be possible if undisturbed patches containing many abalone had been allowed to remain on the seafloor.

The large populations of California groundfish led fisheries managers to believe that the animals produced large numbers of offspring. In reality, the bottom-dwelling fish live up to 140 years, and the large populations represent animals of many different ages. Due to this misconception, managers allowed too many fish to be caught, especially the old fat fish that consumers prefer but that also have the greatest reproductive success. More effective fisheries management would ensure that a significant number of groundfish live to greater maturity.

Limiting the Catch

Fisheries managers often set quotas so that the number of fish caught does not exceed the Maximum Sustainable Yield (MSY). The MSY is the maximum possible number of fish that managers think can be harvested over the long term, including catch plus bycatch. The difficulty calculating the MSY is that there are many unknown quantities; for example, the real number of fish in the fishery, the number of fish that are actually caught, or the number of fish lost as bycatch.

When an MSY for a fishery is determined, managers may reduce the number of boats that are allowed there. In some cases, the government may buy back some of the boats, as was done when the government bought back 35% of the boats that had exploited the California groundfish fishery. Often it is the most damaging boats, such as bottom trawlers, that are eligible for the buy back, which leaves the small-scale fishers to try to make a living in the damaged seas. Fisheries managers may also set size limits on fish, allowing the younger fish to reach sexual maturity. For populations to recover, however, the fish need to be allowed to spawn multiple times.

Another way to limit the catch is to reduce the fishing season. Managers' decisions on how long to allow the fishery to be open are based on several unknowns, including the number of boats that will be fishing and how many fish each boat will catch. Season limits encourage bad practices since fishers need to fish quickly. When season restrictions were attempted on the Alaskan halibut fishery, thousands of boats would try to harvest a year's worth of fish in 48 hours. Fishers fished around the clock, in bad conditions, and took risks with their health, safety, and equipment. Seafood processors could not keep up with the boom and bust cycle.

The Alaskan halibut fishery now works toward sustainability with **individual fish quotas (IFQs)** and an eight-month-long season. With the longer season, fishers no longer take unnecessary risks to themselves, their equipment, or the environment. With IFQs, the total fishing quota is divided into percentage shares that are distributed among all of the fishers using the fishery. Since each shareholder receives a percentage of the total quota, fishers profit by conservation methods that improve the health of the fishery. The quota can be reduced if fisheries managers determine that the current level is damaging the long-term sustainability of the fishery. The number of IFQs an individual can hold is also limited, or the owner of the IFQ must be on the fishing vessel so that one person or organization does not own the entire fishery. The weakness in IFQ plans is that fishers may dump lower value fish so that they can fill their quota with higher value fish, a practice that must be discouraged.

If a fishery is in decline, it may be necessary to place a temporary moratorium on fishing. This has been done with the groundfish fishery off California's continental shelf. If the moratorium is placed after the fishery is economically extinct, though, as with the North Atlantic cod fishery, recovery may not come for decades, if at all.

Reducing Bycatch

Bycatch organisms are undoubtedly important in the marine food web and to other fishers. Reducing bycatch is imperative for maintaining healthy fisheries. Varied limits should be set for different species of bycatch in different locations. Allowable bycatch for an endangered species is zero, but a small amount of bycatch could be allowed for other species. Fishers should be allowed to trade rights to fish, so that captured bycatch are harvested and not thrown back into the sea dead.

Successful techniques for reducing bycatch depend on the species being caught and the fishing method being used. Bottom trawling and other destructive fishing methods should be banned and replaced with new techniques. For example, a device called the Nordmore grate catches shrimp in traps and keeps 98% of unwanted animals caught alive so that they can be released. Turtle exclusion devices are now required of all shrimp trawlers in the United States and in countries that sell wild-caught shrimp to the United States. These devices allow turtles to swim out of trap doors. Such devices should be modified to release other bycatch as well. Gill nets can be set up with electronic beeps to warn away marine mammals. Longlines that attract seabirds can be put out at night when the birds are not active or can be put out with streamers to scare the birds. The lines are less visible to the birds if the bait is dyed blue or the line is reeled out underwater.

Better Management

Many people and organizations have an interest in a fishery, so, to be successful, fisheries management must include all viewpoints. Fishers need to have their economic needs addressed. Fisheries and ecosystem biologists have important data and viewpoints, and environmentalists have the long-term health of the ecosystem in mind. Good fisheries management is based on sound scientific research and honest assessments of fish populations, boat numbers, and fish caught. Instead of reacting to a crisis, as has too often been the case, fisheries managers should be able to anticipate where the problems with a fishery will be, long before a crisis occurs.

Restricting a fishery is never popular with the people and businesses that depend on it to feed their families or to make a profit. But restrictions are more successful if the management plan involves the community. In Port Orford, Oregon, fishers, scientists, and environmentalists are working together to determine their long-term goals for the fishery while deciding on how best to meet the economic requirements of the fishers. The fishers have been driven to make difficult choices by the previous collapse of the salmon fishery and the current problems with the groundfish fishery.

MARINE PROTECTED AREAS

The failure of fisheries managers to adequately protect fisheries and the recognition that entire ecosystems, not just commercially valuable species, deserve protection have led to the creation of **marine protected areas (MPAs)**. Like protected areas on land, MPAs vary in their size, shape, objectives, and types and levels of protection. While all MPAs protect fisheries, some also safeguard ecosystems and other resources, such as cultural treasures and local economies.

There are more than 4,500 MPAs throughout the world, yet they cover less than one percent of the ocean's surface. Many MPAs are small and located in countries where they are not monitored, and where regulations are not enforced. Fisheries may be temporarily or permanently restricted, or they may be closed to some types of fishing gear; to gain fishing industry support, some MPAs have few limits on fishing. MPAs are most successful where they protect a specific habitat, such as a coral reef.

In the United States, MPAs include national marine sanctuaries, some fisheries management areas, national wildlife refuges, and state conservation areas. MPAs totaling more than 7,700 square miles (20,000 square km) have been set up around the collapsed Georges Bank cod fishery. Restrictions include the number of days that the area can be fished and a 40% reduction in trawling. The biomass of some species has increased within some MPAs because there now are more large fish and more young fish. Haddock biomass has increased by more than five times, yellowtail flounder by more than eight times, and scallops by 14 times. Fishers gather just outside the MPAs where the fishing is rich, which may decrease the ability of the MPAs to increase fish populations outside of those jurisdictions.

MARINE RESERVES

Marine reserves are far more restrictive than MPAs. They are listed as "no take" zones; that is, no fishing, energy or mineral extraction, or other habitat-altering activities are allowed in these areas. Resembling wildlife refuges on land, marine reserves protect entire ecosystems, not just economically valuable species of fish. MPAs provide a place for marine life to recover from overfishing and habitat destruction, and may increase fishery yields outside the area. However, as of 2007, only 0.6% of the ocean was fully protected.

No-take reserves have several advantages over MPAs. Marine reserves give shelter to more fish and to more large fish and have greater biodiversity. They provide a place where natural ecosystems can be studied, allowing fisheries managers to more successfully supervise sites outside the reserve. According to Rod Fujita, "catch limits protect 'paper' fish; marine reserves protect real fish." Marine reserves provide an "insurance policy," as Fujita says, against the mistakes of fisheries management. If an area is overfished, or if it is fished badly, as was the white abalone fishery off California, marine preserves provide a bank where the ecosystem and its species are unharmed. Marine reserves provide some economic advantages over MPAs: Marine reserves are more attractive as locations for ecotourists, divers and snorkelers, whale watchers, and other people who are interested in natural systems.

At this time, marine reserves are set up only when there is a crisis. Environmentalists would like to see reserves created much earlier in order to protect a portion of all natural ecosystems. Some advocates suggest that at least 20% of the ocean be set aside permanently. Many marine scientists suggest that reserves be set up adjacent to MPAs with responsible fisheries management so that organisms can move between them. New Zealand and Australia (primarily within the Great Barrier Reef Marine Park) have national networks of marine reserves, and both the Bahamas and Belize are working on establishing some.

Many fishers are skeptical about the value of marine reserves, and in some places there has been a backlash against them. For this reason, among others, scientists and environmentalists recommend that sites be chosen carefully, with the cooperation of fishers, scientists, and environmentalists, and with consideration of local social and economic issues. To be successful, marine reserves must be supported by solid science, effective design, and active community involvement. Good choices for new reserves are locations that would minimize short-term economic impact on fishers; for example, locations that have been fished out but still contain good habitat; or locations that have not been fished yet.

Although most marine reserves are likely to be coastal, "no take" areas could also be set up in the open ocean in locations where fish tend to congregate. The boundaries could be geographical if the location is fixed, for example, off a continental margin, but could be based on migrating factors such as temperature, salinity, or nutrients. These moving reserves would shelter the species that are hardest to protect, such as the large migratory fish that inhabit large portions of the oceans.

POLITICAL ACTION

Little will be done to protect significant areas of the ocean from overfishing without coordinated political action, both nationally and internationally. Scientists and environmentalists suggest the creation of a government council with the mandate to protect ocean ecosystems and species. The ultimate goal of such a council should be sustainable fisheries that include enough adult fish to keep up population numbers. The council would spearhead the creation of marine reserves and set up incentives for preserving ecosystems and fisheries.

WRAP-UP

Marine animals are the only wild animals that continue to be hunted on a large scale, often with very little regulation. In most fisheries, short-term economic gain wins out over long-term sustainability. Marine researchers have developed practices to improve the long-term outlook of fisheries, such as IFQs, which reward fishers for practices that improve the health of a fishery. Most fisheries receive little management until they are in crisis or have collapsed, and no fishery that has collapsed has yet rebounded. To avoid crises, marine reserves should be set up as insurance policies against fisheries mismanagement and for scientific study. If done with the cooperation of all members of the community that have a stake in the reserve—fishers, marine scientists, and the public at large—marine reserves can save ecosystems and provide benefits to the community.

Aquaculture

As the ocean is being fished to its limit and human populations continue to grow, aquaculture has stepped in to produce increasing amounts of seafood. Today, nearly one-third of seafood comes from fish and shellfish farms and that number is growing. Fish farming is an economic asset to developing nations and to coastal regions that have not been attractive to wild fish. But aquaculture facilities are difficult to design and operate, and there are many environmental impacts depending on the species being raised, the structure and mechanics of that particular farm, and the location. Some types of fish farms take eggs and young animals from the seas and return pollutants, such as nutrients and pharmaceuticals.

PROBLEMS WITH AQUACULTURE

Aquaculture projects are prone to technological, economic, and environmental problems. To be successful, the projects must be well planned, designed, and operated. To be sustainable, they must be sensitive to the environment. Since fish farmers are trying to make money, the farms must also be economically viable.

Fish farming is expensive, especially in developed nations, where land and labor costs are high. Costs can be brought down by choosing land wisely and by using machines instead of human laborers. In developing countries, labor is relatively inexpensive, but land prices may be high as coastal cities expand. Because coastal regions are prone to storms, the ponds and cages set up to hold the animals must be able to withstand strong wind, waves, and storm surges even as the cost of constructing and maintaining them is kept reasonable.

Fish farms, especially those raising top predators, need a lot of feed, which must be plentiful, inexpensive, and not consumable by humans. Even then, the overuse of fish protein may weaken the marine food web, as was discussed in the previous chapter regarding Southern Ocean krill. Farmed fish must breed in captivity, something to which some valuable species, such as tuna, are resistant.

Aquaculture has many potential environmental costs. Farmed fish were originally taken from wild stocks, but most are now genetically altered or hybridized to encourage quick growth. If these individuals escape into the wild, they may outcompete the native fish for food resources and be better able to avoid predators. This would change the gene pool of the native population and reduce their genetic variability.

Where fish are closely packed together, excess food and animal wastes will increase the nutrients in the water and cause eutrophication. Technologies have been developed to minimize this problem, but they are expensive. Closely packed animals are prone to disease because pathogens can spread easily among them; nearby wild populations are also more vulnerable. For example, sea lice are small, parasitical crustaceans that create open sores in farmed salmon, affecting their ability to live in salt water. Juvenile wild salmon ordinarily contract a few of these parasites as they swim downriver to the sea. But if the wild fish must swim past a salmon farm, they often become infested and may infect other wild fish at sea. To protect the closely packed animals from the threat of disease, fish farmers release antibiotics into the water. This can affect natural bacterial activity and bring about the evolution of antibiotic-resistant strains of bacteria, possibly affecting wild fish populations and even humans.

Since fish farming is expensive in developed countries, much farmed seafood is imported from developing countries. For example, the top-selling farmed seafood in the United States is large shrimp, or tiger prawns, that are grown in tropical Southeast Asia. The region currently has about 110,000 shrimp farms covering around 3.2 million acres (1.3 million hectares). Globally, shrimp farming is worth about $60 billion. Shrimp farms are a major factor in habitat loss in these regions, displacing mangroves, salt marshes, and freshwater wetlands. Nearly 40% of the decline in mangrove forests is due to shrimp farms. Shrimp farming produces many environmental problems: demand for fish meal to feed farmed shrimp; pollution with chemicals such as antibiotics, pesticides, disinfectants, and fertilizers, some of which bioaccumulate; and eutrophication, due to large amounts of waste. In Thailand alone, the effluent from shrimp farms is about 340 billion gallons (1.3 billion cubic meters). Where shrimp farming is done without environmental safeguards, the ponds must be abandoned in only five or six years due to disease and poor water quality, resulting in the additional loss of coastal habitat.

On the other hand, filter-feeding shellfish—oysters, clams, and mussels—are relatively easy to raise and have minimal environmental impact. Many types of farmed shellfish are beneficial; they clear the water of excess plankton and, since they only grow in nonpolluted water, they inspire people to keep the coastal waters clean. Other good aquacultural practices are discussed in the next section.

GOOD AQUACULTURAL PRACTICES

For aquaculture to be sustainable, it must be done with minimal impact on the environment. Farming native species is often more successful, since the animals are better adapted to the local environment. Farming fish that feed lower on the food chain, including filter-feeding shellfish, consumes a smaller amount of energy than the farmed animals provide. Land must be chosen carefully to minimize impact on the environment. Because about 50% of the world's mangroves have already been destroyed, it is necessary to protect those that remain.

Research is needed to determine the amounts of pollutants, such as nutrients, toxic chemicals, and pathogens, that neighboring ecosystems can absorb. National standards must be set, and individual fish farms must be monitored. Fish feeds must be developed that have less of an environmental impact, such as plant-based feeds that meet the nutritional needs of the farmed fish and of the people who consume them, yet have a minimal impact on the marine environment.

As with farms on land, fish farms can be certified organic. These farms use organic compounds rather than harmful chemicals, and minimize the consumption of fish meal. Since these techniques are more expensive, small farmers need encouragement and financial assistance to convert and maintain their farms.

Polyculture, in which several species of animal are farmed together, is more environmentally sound than monocultures of a single species. Polycultures more closely approach the natural environment; because individuals of the same species are not packed so closely together, polyculture lowers the threat of disease. Polycultures also provide farmers with an economic safeguard if market conditions change and one of the species they are farming is no longer marketable. Polyculture has been practiced in individual fish farms in China for centuries and should be encouraged worldwide.

Aquaculturists must be held accountable for their adherence to environmental regulations. All countries should adhere to the same rules, and nations should be allowed to ban the import of fish and seafood that is farmed in environmentally unsound ways. Consumers should be made aware of how fish are farmed so that they can make sound choices.

In a guest editorial of the December 2003 issue of *World Aquaculture* magazine, Dr. Jane Lubchenco of Oregon State University advocates "sustainable aquaculture," which she says will "require the integration of ecological, social, and economic tradeoffs. Simply producing the best product at the cheapest prices regardless of the environmental or social consequences is not 'sustainable.' Minimizing the consequences of land or sea transformation, minimizing the inputs and outputs as well as their consequences needs to be part of the equations as well."

WHAT SHOULD WE EAT?

Fish and shellfish are an important part of a healthy diet. Because fish is lean and low in saturated fats, the American Heart Association recommends at least two servings of fish per week. Cold-water fish, such as salmon, tuna, rainbow trout, sardines, mackerel, herring, and anchovies, contain omega-3 fatty acids, which have benefits for people with heart and cholesterol problems and rheumatoid arthritis, among other conditions.

Seafood can have adverse health impacts as well, particularly top predators that accumulate toxins to dangerous levels. The Environmental Protection Agency (EPA) and the Food and Drug Administration (FDA) recommend not eating the same kind of fish more than once a week and some fish not more than once a month to avoid ingesting too many of the same toxins. Women of childbearing age and children must be particularly cautious, since compounds like methyl mercury can harm the developing nervous system in a fetus or young child.

Consuming both wild-caught and farmed fish has environmental impacts. Consumers should avoid eating wild-caught fish that have been overfished and should not eat long-lived, deep-water fish unless the fishery has proven to be sustainably managed. Consumers should avoid eating fish that are farmed unsustainably.

The Department of Commerce issues "Dolphin Safe" certification to companies that capture tuna using environmentally responsible methods. *(Courtesy of NOAA)*

Consumers can support fisheries and fish farms that are better for the environment by choosing sustainable, environmentally friendly wild and farmed fish. Some seafood products use "ecolabeling," which lets consumers know if a product has been harvested or grown with an acceptable amount of environmental impact. For example, "dolphin safe" tuna was the first ecolabeling done in the United States. The designation consisted of a label that indicated to consumers that the canned tuna they saw on the shelf had been captured using techniques that did not kill dolphins. In the past few years, other fish products have been ecolabeled to show that the food has been captured in sustainable fisheries. Ecolabels are granted to companies by an independent third-party organization.

Ecolabels are not yet common, and there are several seafood awareness campaigns that list good and bad seafood choices. To get an acceptable rating in one of these campaigns, the fisheries for wild-caught fish must be well managed and fished sustainably, with little bycatch. For aquaculture operations, farms must be well managed with little environmental impact. Some campaigns have prepared health charts on which they recommend maximum safe allowances of particular fish for both adults and children. Links to some of these lists can be found in the "Further Reading/Web Sites" section of this book.

WRAP-UP

As Dr. Jane Lubchenco of Oregon State University says, "Make no mistake: the Blue Revolution has begun and is needed." Fish farms can provide a great deal of animal protein to humans for the indefinite future if they are managed sustainably. They must be designed and managed for long-term use, rather than just for short-term economic gain. Practices such as polyculture and organic farming should be encouraged since they minimize environmental impacts. Consumers can encourage fishers and fish farmers to use sound practices by buying seafood that has been approved by a seafood awareness campaign or that has been ecolabeled.

Marine Mammals

For centuries, marine mammals have been exploited for their fur, oil, and meat. Intense hunting has resulted in enormous population declines for many of these animals. While dolphins were not hunted, they were nevertheless lost in great numbers as bycatch in tuna fishing. Despite protections, two-thirds of marine mammal species globally are now classified as threatened. Hunting has been reduced, or in some cases stopped, but only some populations are recovering. The reasons for this are varied.

WHALING

Whale hunting is hard, dangerous work. Whales are enormous, intelligent creatures that dive deep into the sea beyond the reach of hunters. Some native cultures whaled for thousands of years, and because whale hunting is so difficult, they were able to kill few animals and wasted nothing of the catch. Native whalers ate the meat, used the oil for fuel and light, the bones for tools and construction, and the baleen for structural support.

European cultures were not nearly as resourceful. At the peak of commercial whaling, in the mid-nineteenth century, whales were killed primarily for the oil from their enormous heads, which burned bright, white, and clean in the lamps of the period. This was during the Industrial Revolution, when large increases in the human population and advances in whaling technology brought about the decimation of many species of whales worldwide.

When oil was discovered below ground in Pennsylvania in 1859, the demand for whale oil plummeted—at least in America. Whaling continued in other countries, for oil and then for meat. In the early twentieth century, factory ships were introduced that could process whales incessantly, which led to the need for faster hunting ships and more effective guns. Whaling continued to be important after World War II, when whale oil was an extremely important source of fat in Europe, and whale meat was a valuable part of Japanese and Russian diets.

No one knows how many whales roamed the pre-nineteenth century oceans, but it is estimated that by 1900 there were 4.4 million large whales. The post-World War II era saw the demise of many of the larger whale species, such as the blue whale in the 1940s, the fin and humpback between 1955 and 1970, and the sei whale in later years. As the populations of the mammoth species declined, smaller whales were taken. The paucity of large whales caused Europeans to end whaling in the early 1960s. Japan and the Soviet Union continued to whale as the last of the commercial whale fisheries were depleted. No factory ships sailed after 1978, and by the 1980s the international whale trade was dead, although small-scale coastal whaling continued. The National Marine Fisheries Service (NMFS) of the United States estimates that two million whales were killed by commercial whaling in the twentieth century. Today, eight of the 11 species of commercially hunted whales are commercially extinct; their numbers are so low that it is no longer possible to make money by hunting them.

All commercially valuable whales might be gone were it not for the public outcry. Warnings were sounded in the 1930s that the harvest

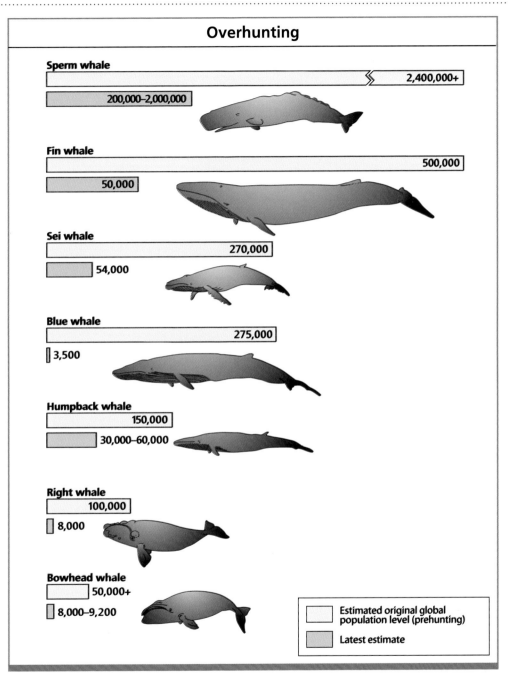

Overhunting

Sperm whale
2,400,000+
200,000–2,000,000

Fin whale
500,000
50,000

Sei whale
270,000
54,000

Blue whale
275,000
3,500

Humpback whale
150,000
30,000–60,000

Right whale
100,000
8,000

Bowhead whale
50,000+
8,000–9,200

Estimated original global population level (prehunting)

Latest estimate

Whales have been hunted commercially for hundreds of years, but rapid declines in numbers of the larger, more valuable species began with the introduction of the exploding harpoon in the 1860s and factory ships in the 1920s. Whales are extremely difficult to count and therefore the numbers presented here are rough estimates.

levels at that time could not be maintained. The International Whaling Commission (IWC) was established in 1946 to manage whale stocks by prohibiting the killing of the most endangered species and limiting the killing of others. Their objective was to "make possible the rational utilization of whale resources in a sustainable manner by conserving the whale stocks for future generations." In 1986, the IWC successfully imposed a moratorium on all commercial whaling.

Whales taken for scientific research are exempt from the IWC moratorium; Japan, where whale meat is a delicacy, has used this exemption as an excuse to continue commercial whaling, mostly of the small and relatively numerous minke whales. Norway resumed whaling in 1993 and has also been increasing the quantity and diversity of the catch. Other countries are considering joining the hunt. According to Whalewatch, Japan, Norway, and Iceland killed over 2,000 whales in 2006 and that number is expected to rise. These countries are now hunting humpback and fin whales and are increasing whaling in Antarctica. Since the whaling ban, nearly 30,000 whales have been killed. Besides research whaling, the IWC allows aboriginal subsistence whaling, provided the population of the hunted whales is not too low. The IWC also sets aside whale sanctuaries. In 1994, they banned whaling entirely from 8 million square miles (21 million square km) around Antarctica, a ban that is now actively ignored by Japan.

Despite the continuation of some whaling, the populations of a few species are rising. The greatest success story has been the eastern Pacific stock of the gray whale, which was removed from the endangered species list in 1993. The population is estimated to be about the same as at the beginning of the nineteenth century, between 17,000 and 23,000 animals, according to NOAA. This number is thought to be the stock's carrying capacity, meaning that it ebbs and flows with the food supply. Unfortunately, the western Pacific stock is still depleted, numbering only in the hundreds. Populations of some whales are still greatly reduced, even after decades of protection. The largest animal that ever lived, the 100-foot (30 m) long blue whale, numbers below 5,000 today (possibly as low as 1,300), down from a prewhaling population estimated at about 275,000.

Even with some populations increasing, antiwhaling sentiment is still high in most countries. Numerous organizations want to continue the ban because of the cruelty that is associated with whale hunting. There is, they say, no way to hunt a large, semisubmerged, air-breathing animal humanely.

SEALS

Seals have long been hunted for their thick, warm fur. By the beginning of the twentieth century, the populations of several species were reduced to dangerously low numbers. Initially, quotas were enacted in the United States and were somewhat effective, but protections became much stronger with the passage of the 1972 Marine Mammals Protection Act.

Protection has contributed to the population growth of many seal species. The population of Guadalupe fur seals (*Arctocephalus townsendi),* found only on Guadalupe Island, off Baja California, Mexico, was down to seven animals in 1892. At about the same time, the last eight known Northern elephant seals (*Mirounga angustirostris*) were collected by the Smithsonian Institution, but fortunately, another, unknown population of about 400 was later discovered. From those seven individuals, the Guadalupe fur seal population is now up to about 1,500 animals, and elephant seals are so abundant that they're sometimes found in Southern California swimming pools.

The increase in some species has caused fishers and others to ask for protections to be removed. Harbor seals rob the nets of commercial fishers, yet the fishers are not permitted to harm the animals; they are only allowed to discourage them. Fishers complain that sea lions feed heavily on salmon (also much reduced in number), which return to rivers to spawn. The use of loud noises or trap-and-release programs fails to discourage the sea lions.

Unfortunately, some seal populations that were thought to have recovered have again started to decline. The population of Northern fur seals on Pribilof Island, Alaska, estimated at 23 million in 1867, grew from 300,000 in 1910 to more than one million today. However, the numbers have been decreasing since the mid-1950s, likely due to the reduction in the fish the seals eat and their entanglement in plastic nets, lines, and soft drink rings. Disease and pollution also eradicate seal populations.

Although the seal hunt is off in the United States and many other countries, the hunt continues in a few nations, most notably Canada. In spring 2006, 335,000 North Atlantic harp seal pups were slaughtered in Canada's commercial seal hunt, about one-third of all the pups born. (Dead seal pups are skinned and their fur is sold for coats.) Public outrage nearly ended the hunt in the 1980s (only 15,000 were killed in 1985), but since 1996, the quota has been increasing. Reasons for the increase include fishers' concerns that the seals are eating too many Atlantic cod (an adult seal eats about one ton (900 kg) of sea creatures over its lifetime), plus concerns about the economic well-being of the coastal communities that have already been slammed by the collapse of the cod fishery. New markets for

The Marine Mammal Protection Act of 1972

The precipitous decline of marine mammal populations, the threat of species extinction, and photos of cute baby seals being slaughtered led to an outcry in many nations. In 1972, the United States established the Marine Mammal Protection Act, which bans taking (harvesting, hunting, capturing, or killing, or attempting to kill) or importing any marine mammals or products made from them in the nation's territorial waters and fisheries. The act also makes it unlawful for any person or vessel subject to U.S. jurisdiction to harvest any marine mammals on the high seas, except with a preexisting international treaty. The two exceptions are governed by strict guidelines: A few marine mammals can be caught for scientific research and public display, and a few can be caught by Alaskan natives for food and handicrafts. The act bans the importation of marine mammals and marine mammal products into the United States. Species or stocks must not be allowed to fall below their optimum sustainable population level, and, if they do, measures should be taken to replenish the stock.

the fur have developed in Russia, Ukraine, Poland, and China.

Public pressure has brought about changes in the Canadian hunt since the 1970s. The youngest pups, those with white fur, are off limits. Pups that are three weeks old, with black spotted silvery fur, are now the most desired. Although the seal pups are still clubbed, they are no longer skinned alive. Other species of seals and sea lions are hunted in Canada and other countries. Some seal species cannot be sold due to their endangered status. Some countries are working at the other end of the supply chain to ban the products of the hunt.

A seal pup is about to be clubbed during a hunt in Canada. (© IFAW International Fund for Animal Welfare/S. Cook—www.ifaw.org)

SEA OTTERS

California sea otters have a similar history to that of seals. Scientists estimate that only 300 years ago, more than 500,000 otters lived around the rim of the Pacific Ocean. The California coast, with its small isolated beaches, was home to 20,000 subspecies. By the early 1900s, hunters had wiped out all but a few small populations of the California and Alaskan sea otters. Hunting was banned in 1911, and the Alaskan population has largely recovered. The California population has slowly increased over the past few decades but has now leveled off at about 2,800 animals, likely due to terrestrial parasites.

The loss of the otters has weakened the kelp ecosystem in which they live. Otters love to feast on sea urchins, spiny, hard-shelled animals that eat away at the thick patches of kelp. If hungry otters do not keep urchin populations in check, the urchins overgraze the kelp—creating a barren wasteland on the seafloor. Many of California's kelp forests are suffering because sea otter populations are down. If California sea otters disappear entirely, it could forever change the kelp forest ecosystem.

DOLPHINS

The killing of dolphins and porpoises is different from that of other marine mammals since the animals are not actively hunted but usually die as bycatch, particularly in tuna nets. Due to changes in fishing practices, dolphin deaths have greatly declined. This has become one of the true success stories of the environmental movement.

The dolphins become bycatch in the eastern tropical Pacific (but nowhere else) when mature yellowfin tuna form their schools beneath areas where dolphins swim. When dolphins come to the surface to breathe air, they are spotted by fishers, who use the dolphins to locate the tuna. The fishers then put a purse seine net around the tuna school and haul up whatever is in it; the catch sometimes includes hundreds of dolphins. Over nearly 50 years, roughly 7 million dolphins died this way—about 500,000 annually during peak years.

After publication of appealing photos of dolphins and descriptions of their horrendous mortality rate caused a public outcry, American tuna companies struck an agreement in 1990 to buy only tuna that was caught using dolphin-safe methods. Dolphin-safe tuna is fished in three ways: Fishers use methods other than dolphin-spotting to locate the tuna; they capture the tuna using methods other than purse-seine nets; or they allow dolphins who become trapped in the nets to escape. By 1999, fewer than 3,000 dolphins were dying each year due to tuna fishing.

Despite the change, two species of dolphins, the northern spotted and the eastern spinner, still total only 20% and 30% of their prehunt numbers, respectively. The reasons that the populations have not recovered are unclear. Possibly, more dolphins are killed as bycatch than are being reported, or the stress the dolphins suffer while being rounded up and released reduces their survival or reproduction rates. Fishing practices may still cause harm to the dolphins by separating suckling calves from their mothers or by breaking up dolphin schools.

MANATEES

Manatees are endangered due to habitat loss, pollution, run-ins with solid waste, and increased numbers of red tides. Yet their largest losses, at least in Florida, are sustained due to collisions with motor boats that travel too quickly, catching the slow-moving animals in their propellers. The Florida Manatee Sanctuary Act of 1978 protects Florida manatees from intentional or accidental harm; breaking this law may result in fines and imprisonment. The Florida Manatee Recovery Plan, developed due to the Endangered Species Act, is working toward increasing manatee numbers. The State of Florida is trying to enforce safe boat speeds in locations frequented by manatees, and also to develop local manatee protection plans.

MARINE MAMMAL STRANDINGS

Marine mammals sometimes beach, or strand, themselves when they are ill or stressed by something in their environment. Many of these stranded animals die; many others die at sea and are washed ashore. According to the National Marine Fisheries Service stranding networks, on average, 3,600 marine mammals were stranded each year during the 1990s. Many strandings are of a single animal, but sometimes a whole group is stranded. In one recent incident in the United States, 700 dead bottlenose dolphins washed up on the mid-Atlantic coastline. In another incident, dozens of California sea lions had seizures and died on a public beach. One year, 273 gray whales were found dead on their migration route between Mexico and Alaska; 377 were found dead the following year.

Strandings have many possible causes, including toxins from harmful algal blooms, infectious diseases, malnutrition, and loud, human-generated noises. The cause of any one stranding is often difficult to determine because the animal sometimes is too decomposed for a good autopsy. Of particular concern is the mid-frequency sonar used by the United States Navy to locate so-called silent submarines, which is as loud as a jet engine at its source. These sound waves travel hundreds of miles through the ocean to search for potentially dangerous objects, but for marine mammals they are noise pollution.

Autopsies of some animals that have stranded themselves during or just after military operations involving intense sonar in a narrow region have shown clear damage to their auditory systems or other physical signs of stress. The sounds also scare or disorient other animals, which may cause them to surface too quickly and experience decompression sickness. Known as "the bends" in humans, this condition is instigated by the release of nitrogen gas from the blood into body tissues, small veins, and arteries. The resultant drop in circulating oxygen brings on shock, collapse, or death.

The United States Navy says that there is only one solid link between a stranding and a naval operation. In 2000, in the Bahamas, five United States Naval ships were using mid-frequency sonar in a restricted area. Fourteen beaked whales, two minke whales, and one spotted dolphin were trapped in a boxed canyon, could not escape the sound, and beached themselves. Seven of the beached whales died and the rest were pushed live back into the water, but no one knows their fate. Four of those autopsied had unusual hemorrhages near and around their ears, consistent with injuries expected from exposure to loud noise. Environmental scientists cite many other examples, but the Navy is not convinced. While the United States Navy's use of mid-frequency sonar has been restricted, other countries are developing the technology.

Noise may have more subtle effects on marine mammals. Unknown sounds may hinder their ability to follow migratory routes, locate each other, find food, or care for their young. Naval sonar can cause humpback whales to alter their songs, orcas to disrupt their feeding, and porpoises and other species to leap from the water or flee the area in order to escape the sounds.

WRAP-UP

Marine mammals are intelligent, appealing animals that have suffered enormous population declines at human hands in the past two centuries. Many species were hunted to near extinction for their oil or meat. Marine mammals are now protected, and the populations of many species are increasing, although rising populations are leading to pressure from whaling and sealing nations to increase hunting once again. However, some species do not seem to be recovering; the reasons are varied and include continued hunting, environmental stress, and disease. In cases where populations are not increasing as was hoped, research must be done into the cause, and action should be taken to protect the animals.

Habitat Destruction

Marine habitats are destroyed for many reasons, primarily through development, pollution, and harmful fishing techniques. The most threatened marine habitats are near coastlines, where landscapes are converted to urban, agricultural, or aquacultural uses. Out from the shore, tropical coral reefs are damaged by pollution, harmful fishing practices, and other human activities. Even habitats in the deep sea—at seamounts, for example—are threatened by pollution and overfishing. This chapter surveys habitat destruction of marine environments from the coast to the deep sea.

BEACHES

Beaches are the sites for many recreational activities, both onshore and offshore. Beaches also protect the inland areas behind them from coastal erosion, provided they themselves do not erode away. Human activities are now causing about 70% of the world's beaches to erode faster than normal. In one costly mistake, groins constructed to save a building at

Cape Hatteras, North Carolina, robbed sand from below the lighthouse, requiring that building to be relocated—at a cost of $12 million.

In developed countries, heroic efforts may be undertaken to preserve a beach. The U.S. Army Corps of Engineers has replenished some beaches by dredging sand from channels or offshore, transporting it to the beach, and shaping it into a beach form. Beach replenishment can cost millions of dollars, and the beach likely will be depleted of sand again in several years—or even sooner if there is a hurricane or other large storm. Taxpayers are beginning to revolt at the expense, saying that people should not be allowed to build so close to beaches; but leaders of coastal communities respond by pointing out that sandy beaches have aesthetic, recreational, and economic values that tourists enjoy.

Beach pollution is a growing problem, but the situation with some pollutants is improving. Less sewage is entering coastal waters because of upgraded treatment plants and long pipes that discharge sewage farther offshore. More cities are diverting roadway runoff to sewage treatment plants. The problem is getting worse with some pollutants though, specifically fertilizers, and animal and pet waste. Each year in the United States, there are more than 4,500 swimming advisories and temporary beach closings, usually from bacterial outbreaks. Despite this large number, U.S. beaches are heavily monitored and regulated; as a result, they are among the cleanest in the world.

Coastal communities must grow in ways that not only benefit people but also leave some habitat untouched. To ease the impact of development on the coastal environment, previously used land should be reused, and air and water pollution should be limited. Regulating growth requires careful management plans and the cooperation of business, political, scientific, and environmental leaders.

COASTAL WETLANDS

Half of the world's coastal wetlands have been lost to development and aquaculture. In the United States, wetlands destruction traditionally stemmed from the seemingly endless landscape of swamps

Outer Banks, North Carolina

The greatest barrier island system in the world is found along the Outer Banks of North Carolina. Under natural conditions, storm waters would bring sand over the islands and into the lagoons to create marshes, causing the barrier islands to move slightly landward. But heavy development and Highway 12, which runs along the length of the barrier island system, must be protected. Engineers have constructed a 50-mile-long artificial dune that blocks the sand from moving in all but the largest storms. When storm waters deposit sand on the highway, road maintenance crews pile it into unnatural dunes, rather than allowing it to go over the islands. Since sediment is no longer being replenished, the marsh is sinking.

When Hurricane Isabel struck this region in September 2003, Highway 12 broke up in places, beaches eroded, and a new 1,700 foot (520 m) wide inlet sliced across Hatteras Island, cutting the village of Hatteras off from the rest of the island. Although the creation of inlets is a natural process on barrier islands, community leaders concerned about tourism—the region's only industry—would not entertain the idea of leaving the inlet open. To fix the problem, a pipe was laid underwater, and sand was pumped from the nearby sound into the inlet, at a cost of about $5 million.

09/08/1999, Before

09/21/2003, After

Hatteras Island before and after Hurricane Isabel in 2003. The island has been breached in several places, and the road has been destroyed. Some buildings have disappeared. (US Geological Survey)

and a lack of understanding of the important role wetlands play. The federal Arkansas Act of 1850 and the Green Act of 1868 essentially instructed the states to convert wetlands into ports, harbors, rail lines, roads, and agricultural and recreational lands—and that is what the states did.

The U.S. Congress has, however, also acted to protect wetlands. Wetlands are only supposed to be developed if all other possibilities have been exhausted. Developers must also replace the wetlands they destroy. However, few projects are ever turned down, and replacement wetlands are often far away or of poor quality. The result is that enormous areas of wetlands are still being lost in places like Florida where, between 1993 and 2003, 61,000 acres (250 square km) of wetlands were filled, although the rate of loss appears to be decreasing more recently.

Other countries are decimating wetlands as well. Globally, 35% to 50% of mangroves have been lost, including 25% of those in Malaysia and 50% of those in Thailand. An estimated 62 million acres (25 million hectares) of mangrove forest have been destroyed or grossly degraded in the past century. Wetlands loss shrinks fish, shellfish, and bird populations. Half of the world's wading bird populations are in decline. Birds that live in large flocks will not breed if their population goes too low, and 28% of shorebirds are approaching such numbers. Without wetlands, migratory birds lose places to stop over during their long migrations. The governments of Canada and the United States noticed in the 1970s that the migrating population of waterfowl had dropped from hundreds of millions to a few million. In 1986, the North American Waterfowl Management Plan was formed to protect and restore wetlands along migratory routes; Mexico joined in 1989. In one project, volunteers sowed 23 tons (21,000 kg) of grass seed in mudflats around Arkansas's Big Lake. The next winter, the lake attracted almost a million ducks, 30 times the number that had shown up the previous year.

Wetlands also play an important role in protecting inland areas from acts of nature, such as hurricanes and tsunamis.

Protected by Nature

Mangroves, coral reefs, and sand dunes protect the land behind them from storm surge and other rapid sea level increases. Experts say that the Boxing Day 2004 tsunami would have been less destructive had the natural barriers that protect coastlines remained.

When the tsunami struck, communities that were behind natural barriers suffered much less than those that had eliminated them. Mangrove forests in Thailand, vegetated sand dunes in Sri Lanka's national parks, and coral reefs in the Maldives all protected their inland communities. The tsunami caused its worst damage where mangroves had been cleared and where beaches had previously eroded due to coral reef damage.

A team of researchers from the United States and Sri Lanka, led by Harindra Fernando of Arizona State University, studied an area of Sri Lanka where a 30-foot (20 m) wave swept one mile (1.5 km) inland, carrying a passenger train 200 feet (50 m) off its tracks and resulting in 1,700 deaths. At this location, the coral reefs had been decimated by illegal mining, including the use of explosives to harvest coral and fish. In *EOS*, the newspaper of the American Geophysical Union, Fernando and his team wrote in August 2005, "Through hundreds of eyewitness accounts, diver observations and wave measurements, it was possible to conclude that illeg al coral mining along unsupervised beaches had

WETLANDS RESTORATION: SAN FRANCISCO BAY

After over a century of wetlands loss, a few communities have begun wetlands restoration projects. The most extensive is in San Francisco Bay, California, the most modified estuarine system in the United States. Before the California Gold Rush in 1849, the bay supported 540 square miles (1,400 square km) of freshwater wetlands and 310 square miles (800 square km) of salt marshes; only about 5%, or 48 square miles (125 square km), of both environments now remain. The bay's remaining wetlands make up 90% of California's current total and provide a crucial stop for migrating and wintering waterfowl and a home for many organisms.

For decades, the bay has been filled to provide foundations for major cities and to create ponds for salt production. But when developers proposed taking down a major mountain to fill in more of the created defenseless 'low resistance paths' that allowed focused water jetting into the land and intensified destruction."

Just 2 miles (3 km) to the south of this destruction, where the coral reefs are protected and nurtured for the tourist trade, the wave was only 7 to 10 feet (2 to 3 m) high and traveled just 200 feet (50 m) inland with no fatalities. Eyewitnesses described a visible reduction in the height of the water wall of as much as 80% to 95% that researchers conclude was caused by the reef. Although the Maldives islands were directly in the tsunami's path, they escaped destruction because they are surrounded by healthy coral reefs. The reefs themselves mostly survived the tsunami unharmed, except where they were struck by debris, but mangroves were damaged in some locations; for example, 100 square miles (250 square km) of mangroves were damaged in Indonesia.

Seeing the relation between marine habitat destruction and the effects of the tsunami has prompted some of these governments to work toward restoring their coastlines. Indonesia plans to replant at least 75,000 acres (30,000 hectares) of mangroves in its hardest hit areas, and Malaysia plans to protect its remaining mangroves. Sri Lanka is considering protecting mangroves and dunes and requiring developers to build artificial reefs for their projects.

bay in the 1960s, the public rebelled, and a commission charged with preserving and protecting the region was established. Since then, only a small amount of fill has been allowed and that lost habitat has been replaced with an equal or greater amount of wetlands elsewhere.

With a population of more than seven million people, the San Francisco Bay region has tremendous runoff. Shipping and industry are vital economic forces. The bay and its sediments are heavily polluted with pesticides, heavy metals, and other pollutants. Shellfish in the South Bay are so full of heavy metals that migrating birds are at risk of being poisoned. Human activities have caused native fish and wildlife populations to plummet, and the bay supports 50 threatened and endangered species. Even the salt ponds, which are not a natural part of the environment, are home to more than 30 special-status species.

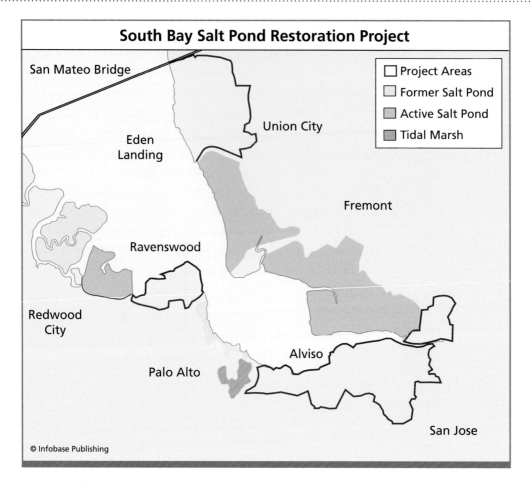

South Bay Salt Pond Restoration Project

San Mateo Bridge

Eden
Landing

Union City

Fremont

Ravenswood

Redwood
City

Palo Alto

Alviso

San Jose

Legend:
- Project Areas
- Former Salt Pond
- Active Salt Pond
- Tidal Marsh

© Infobase Publishing

South San Francisco Bay south of the San Mateo Bridge. The three sets of salt ponds slated for restoration as part of the South Bay Salt Pond Restoration Project are shown in red.

To undo some of the damage that has been done, the South Bay Salt Pond Restoration Project is set to convert 25 square miles (65 square km) of commercial salt ponds in the South Bay region back into wetlands. The project's aims are to restore a mix of wetland habitats, including tidal marshes and managed ponds; supply flood management in the South Bay; and provide wildlife-oriented recreational activities to the public. The tidal marshes will provide nurseries and living space for fish, shorebirds, water birds, and harbor seals. The salt ponds will serve as stopping points for 20 species of birds.

Restoration will be difficult. Exotic species have driven some native species from their homes and have increased predation on others. Bay sediments are full of mercury and the bacteria that convert it to harmful methyl mercury. Over the years, the salt ponds have sunk, and it will be difficult to find clean enough sediment to raise the newly created wetlands. Of course, it is only because the salt ponds are there that there is land available for wetlands restoration. As a result, a project of this magnitude is unlikely to be duplicated elsewhere.

CORAL REEFS

In August 1996, President Bill Clinton said, "Pollution, overfishing, and overuse have put many of our unique reefs at risk. Their disappearance would destroy the habitat of countless species. It would unravel the web of marine life that holds the potential for new chemicals, new medicines, and unlocking new mysteries. It would have a devastating effect on the coastal communities from Cairns to Key West, Florida—communities whose livelihood depends upon the reefs."

Coral reefs are both sensitive and resilient—they can be pounded by cyclonic storms and yet will recover. However, coral reefs are not resilient to chronic disturbances such as pollution and high temperatures. According to Dr. Clive Wilkinson, coordinator of the Global Coral Reef Monitoring Network, 20% of coral reefs are severely damaged and unlikely to recover, while 24% are at imminent risk of collapse. Only 40% are at low risk from human pressures, except for global climate change, which can damage all reefs everywhere. When coral reefs die, so does the diverse ecosystem that they support.

Damaged coral reefs often turn white, a phenomenon called **coral bleaching**. Coral bleaching is a relatively new problem—it was first recognized in 1983—but it has become common. When coral animals are stressed, they expel their zooxanthellae. Since these algae give the coral its color, only the rocky part of the reef, the white limestone, is left, with a thin cover of transparent tissue. If a coral polyp loses its zooxanthellae for too long, the coral starves and the reef dies. Sometimes zooxanthellae move back in when conditions improve. Coral

Coral that has lost its zooxanthellae also loses its color and becomes bleached. One likely cause of coral bleaching is increased sea surface temperatures. This coral was photographed off of Moorea Island in French Polynesia. *(Alexis Rosenfeld/Photo Researchers)*

reefs may recover from one bleaching event, but multiple events can kill them.

Wilkinson's report, *Status of Coral Reefs of the World: 2004* blames coral bleaching on rising seawater temperatures caused by global warming. Coral polyps are very temperature sensitive, and an increase in a summer maximum temperature of only 1.8°F (1°C) for two to three days can trigger a coral bleaching event. If the elevated temperatures persist for less than one month, the reef will likely recover, but sustained heat causes irreversible damage.

An extensive and severe bleaching occurred in 1998 when an El Niño event (followed by an equally strong La Niña) caused temperatures at the sea surface to rise to their highest levels in modern times. Wilkinson says that about 16% of the world's reefs in oceans and seas—including the Pacific, Indian, Red Sea, Persian Gulf, Mediterranean, and Caribbean—were damaged. Reef mortality was greater than 70% in some locations in the Indian Ocean. In East Africa, the Arabian Persian Gulf, the Maldives, Palau, and Japan, warmer temperatures killed some 1,000-year-old corals. Yet within six years, Wilkinson found that 40% of the damaged reefs had recovered. In some of the healed reefs, the resident zooxanthellae were replaced by a more heat-tolerant species.

Sediment runoff kills reefs because the zooxanthellae cannot photosynthesize in cloudy water and dirt may clog the coral polyps' breathing pores in their skin. Deforestation of nearby inland areas increases both sedimentation and freshwater runoff, since the rain no longer seeps into the soil of those areas. The addition of freshwater lowers seawater salinity, another problem for coral polyps. Windblown dust from Africa has damaged reefs in the Caribbean and Florida by blocking sunlight and by bringing in pesticides or toxic fungi that have adhered to the dust granules. Although such an effect has not yet been seen in nature, increasing ocean acidity could damage coral reefs. For example, laboratory and field experiments have shown that some coral and other reef organisms produce less calcium carbonate in seawater that contains double the current amount of CO_2—a level that is predicted to be reached in 50 years.

Coral polyps that are stressed from elevated temperatures or pollution are more susceptible to diseases. Many reefs currently exhibit infections, tumors, and lesions. These features were not seen until recently and do not appear in photos going back to the 1930s. Reef fish and invertebrates living in stressful environments may also be more susceptible to diseases. Stress also decreases the ability of reefs to survive events such as tropical storms, floods, and volcanic eruptions—events the reefs have coped with for millions of years.

Overfishing is a problem for reef fish, which are caught for either food or the aquarium trade. The introduction of new types of gear has made fishing easier: Nylon nets are cheap, and fishers are able to buy larger nets and use them for many years. They also use nylon and other synthetics to build fish traps. Outboard motors allow fishers to

Snails at Risk

Some invertebrate populations are declining precipitously, including cone snails, which live in coral reefs or mangrove swamps. The 500 species of cone snails have beautifully colored and patterned shells that are sold to tourists in seaside resorts.

Cone snails are deadly, injecting venom into their prey through a hollow tooth. So that the prey cannot become adapted to the poison, each species has as many as 100 varieties of toxin strong enough to paralyze or kill a person. The enormous variety of toxins, about 50,000 in all, makes cone snails the most important source in nature for potential new pharmaceuticals. So far, scientists have identified compounds that could be used to treat chronic pain, cancer, autoimmune diseases, epilepsy, and clinical depression. To date, most of the research has involved only three cone snail species and a tiny percentage of the total toxins.

No cone snail species are known to have gone extinct, but because the species live in limited ranges, habitat loss could result in their extinction. Currently, 70% of cone snail species are experiencing serious habitat loss. Scientists argue that this group should be protected by forcing countries to monitor and limit exploitation.

reach and harvest fish on remote reefs that once served as the source of new larvae. In the past, when a reef's fish population fell too low, the remaining fish could hide in the reef. The lack of fish would force the fisher to go elsewhere, giving the reef's remaining fish population time to recover. Nowadays, dive masks, night lights, and other tools allow a fisher to catch every last fish on the reef. Refrigeration has expanded the market for reef fish well beyond the distance of an easy boat trip, with the result that more reef fish are now being caught for food.

Some fishing practices damage the reef itself. For example, fishers throw dynamite onto the reef and then collect the dead fish when they rise to the surface; but large numbers of fish and turtles are lost. The dynamite also blows apart a portion of the reef. Divers use another technique where they squirt sodium cyanide solution at a fish to stun it and then collect it. The sodium cyanide also kills the reef, which will then be taken over by seaweed. Reef invertebrates such as cone snails are also at risk from this practice.

Tourists can damage reefs, even as they enjoy their beauty. Reefs are torn up by dive boat anchors and by divers standing on the reefs. Tourists collect or buy coral to take home as souvenirs, often as jewelry. Their desire for fresh seafood increases fishing pressure on nearby reefs, and the effluent from tourist hotels pollutes them.

Once damaged, a coral reef does not recover easily. Some organisms may thrive in the altered environment; plagues of the crown-of-thorns starfish feed on live corals, which then crumble to rubble. Altered habitats are also attractive to invasive species, and seaweed may coat stressed reefs.

It may be difficult for people to let a reef recover. For example, people who live at a subsistence level must catch fish to survive. To find fish when the numbers decrease, the fishers may buy improved gear but then must capture more fish to pay for it. The loss of a reef habitat represents a tremendous economic loss to the people who depend on it for food or income.

With assaults coming from so many sides, what can be done to save coral reefs? Damaging activities must be stopped. Pressures to provide reef fish for food must be reduced, as must pollution. More areas should be designated as no-take marine reserves, and environmentally sustainable tourism must be promoted. And the list goes on. Perhaps the most important action is to reduce greenhouse gas emissions.

A major new initiative in coral reef conservation is designation of 33% of the Great Barrier Reef as no-take zones. These zones encompass 70 different habitats. This action could set a precedent for other areas to conserve their coral reefs.

DEEP SEA SEAMOUNTS

The decline in fish populations near coasts and in shallow water has prompted fishers to look to the deep sea coral reef habitats located on seamounts for their catches. At these depths, bottom trawling is the preferred method of fishing, but the destruction of the sea bottom is especially harmful because the slow-growing, deepwater corals may take decades or even centuries to return to their original condition.

Deepwater fish are slow-growing and long-lived so it is difficult for populations to recover if they are overfished. One example is the orange roughy that lives in the deep sea far offshore. That fishery was exploited for a decade until scientists discovered that the roughy can live for 150 years and takes 25 to 30 years to reach sexual maturity. By the time this was understood, the fish population may have decreased beyond its ability to recover. Some environmental groups are calling for an immediate end to harvesting the orange roughy. New Zealand fish managers respond by saying that long-lived deepwater fish can be harvested sustainably, and that with responsible fishing, some stocks have been recovering. Many countries and scientists agree that deep-ocean corals and sponges must be protected. These conservationists are asking the UN and other international bodies to place a moratorium on bottom trawling on the high seas until the reefs are better understood.

WRAP-UP

Marine habitats are being altered or destroyed worldwide. Habitats are lost to development or aquaculture; some become so polluted that natural systems are compromised. Ambitious restoration projects, like those taking place in San Francisco Bay, must counter the effects of land loss, land sinking, chemical pollutants, heavy metals, and introduced species. These projects are necessary to reclaim land for wildlife, such as the migrating waterfowl that depend on San Francisco Bay for sustenance as other habitats continue to be lost to them. Coral reefs and deepwater reefs are very sensitive to habitat losses and must be protected.

PART FIVE

PROTECTING
THE OCEANS

The Future of
the Oceans

As summarized by Dr. Carl Safina, president of the Blue Ocean Institute, in *Issues in Science and Technology* (2006), "The oceans are in serious trouble; there is an urgent need for action; and the United States needs to significantly revise its policies related to oceans." This chapter outlines some of the changes that need to be made by the United States and other nations and by individuals to protect the world's oceans.

REGULATING THE OCEANS

Laws meant to protect the oceans, passed by the United States and by nations and other bodies around the world, have been discussed in relevant sections throughout this volume. Two points may be obvious: First, there is no all-encompassing conservation policy for the oceans, either nationally or internationally. Current laws provide protection on single issues and were usually enacted to deal with a specific crisis. The Endangered Species Act, for example, was enacted when it was realized that the populations of some bird species were being decimated. While the law did what it set out to do—protect individual species—it cannot be used to protect an entire ecosystem. Second, many conservation laws were enacted in the 1970s when the environmental movement was young and scientific knowledge was much patchier than it is today. New knowledge has changed the way scientists think of ocean protection, and research on species and ecosystems has become a fundamental part of any new protection plan. Clearly, the piecemeal approach now in place has not worked very well, considering the losses in species and habitats that have occurred during the past few decades.

PUBLIC POLICY RECOMMENDATIONS

In 2003, two American commissions issued reports that dealt comprehensively with ocean and coastal protection while focusing primarily on the Exclusive Economic Zone (EEZ) of the United States. The Pew Oceans Commission report focused mostly on living resources, and the United States Commission on Ocean Policy report dealt with living and nonliving resources. The Food and Agricultural Organization of the United Nations' 2006 report on The State of World Fisheries and Aquaculture (SOFIA) took a more international view of ocean health. These reports generally agree on what is needed to improve the health of the oceans, and their public policy recommendations are reviewed below.

Because ocean policy is fragmented and scattered among several different agencies, the major suggestion of both U.S. reports is that the United States establish a single agency or council to develop and coordinate ocean policy. Scientific research would be the basis for this national policy, which would have the goal of protecting the health of marine ecosystems and developing the sustainable use of ocean resources. SOFIA recommends the establishment of a similar international agency.

Fisheries management policies would be based on sound scientific information and would protect entire ecosystems, not just commercially valuable species. These policies could be assessed by independent scientists, who would provide sound data and who would have no financial stake in the exploitation of marine resources. Aquaculture should also be regulated for environmental health. Significantly, virtually all marine scientists advocate setting up extensive networks of marine reserves. Fish stocks should be regulated by regional organizations governed by international guidelines.

The reports recommend better management of coastal development. For financial reasons, development should not be allowed in hazard-prone areas such as floodplains and high-erosion areas. For biological reasons, coastal habitat should be protected and restored. Healthy coastal habitat also safeguards inland areas from storm surge and waves. The moratorium on offshore oil and gas leasing should continue until there is a full understanding of the long-term environmental effects of oil and gas production. Energy sources such as methane hydrates, wind, waves, and ocean thermal energy must be developed fairly and with long-term environmental health in mind.

Both land- and ocean-based sources of pollutants should be better controlled. Allowable pollutant levels should be determined for all sources, including runoff from the land, runoff from ships at sea, airborne pollutants, and discharged ballast water. The enormous problem of excess nutrients should be solved by reducing nutrient use and by improving nutrient removal in wastewater treatment plants. States should receive penalties for not achieving water quality standards. Imports of potentially invasive species must be tracked and their spread prevented.

The United States should become a leader in international ocean management. To do so, it must first ratify the 1982 UN Convention on the Law of the Sea. As the world's foremost greenhouse gas emitter, the United States must act to lower its contribution to global warming. While there is a need to know more about the oceans than ever before, the amount of money spent on ocean research has decreased. Both U.S. commission reports recommend doubling the amount of money spent on ocean research.

People should be educated on the ocean's wonders and on the damage that is being done so that they develop a sense of stewardship for the marine realm. A new ocean ethic should be adhered to which recognizes that the oceans have limits on the resources that they can provide and the waste products that they can accept.

MAKING A DIFFERENCE TO THE OCEANS

The problems of the oceans are enormous, and long-term solutions will take the concentrated efforts of all nations. Meanwhile, through his or her actions, each human being can help to worsen or improve the state of the oceans. Here are some actions both individuals and families can take to minimize human impact on the oceans:

- Do not pour oil or toxic chemicals down the drain or into the sewer.
- Eliminate or reduce pesticide and fertilizer use and use phosphate-free detergent.
- Dispose of garbage properly; recycle as much as possible.
- Try to consume fish and seafood that have been fished or farmed sustainably. If possible, choose products packaged with an ecolabel or that have been listed as safe by the Blue Ocean Institute ("Guide to Ocean Friendly Seafood"), Environmental Defense ("Oceans Alive"), and the Monterey Bay Aquarium ("Seafood Watch Program"). Links to these organizations can be found in the Further Reading/Web Sites section in the back of this volume.
- Do not collect or remove live organisms from the sea unless they are being harvested sustainably. Do not buy jewelry or animal shells that may have been collected from wild organisms that are being overharvested. For example, avoid coral jewelry, coral aquarium decorations, and cone snail shells.
- Be certain that aquarium fish were raised for aquarium purposes or harvested in an environmentally friendly manner.

Try to buy fish with the "Marine Aquarium Council Certified Organisms" label.

⊕ Enjoy the beach, but with as little impact as possible. Obey signs regarding motor vehicles on or near beaches. Stay off sand dunes, which are often fragile ecosystems. Do not harass birds, turtles, or other animals that might live there. In the water, keep away from marine mammals so that they can live and breed without disruption. While boating, obey speed limits. While diving or snorkeling, do not touch, walk on, or collect coral from reefs.

⊕ Do not dump aquarium contents into outdoor water sources. Live aquarium contents should be donated to another aquarium or placed in the garbage, not in the water. Bait buckets too, particularly those containing live fish, should not be emptied into a different body of water from where the bait came from. Boats, scuba gear, and other equipment must be dried off before being moved from one water body to another. Small larvae can be transferred from one water body to another without anyone seeing them, but they cannot live without water.

Everyone can help to decrease the impact people are having on the oceans by being conscious of the choices they make. To have a greater effect, the United States and other nations should follow the recommendations outlined in various reports over the past several years. Good ocean stewardship will be essential in the coming years if catastrophic changes are to be avoided.

Conclusion

Much of what goes on in the sea is mysterious. The oceans are vast, deep, and difficult to study. Scientists use every tool they have—from technologically sophisticated satellites and remotely operated vehicles to primitive collection bottles—to gain knowledge. However, as oceanographers say, we know more about the dark side of the Moon than about our planet's oceans. Much of the information that has been gathered is well-founded, but some is little more than a guess; for example, no one knows the actual numbers of fish that make up a midlevel fishery. Interpretations of scientific information may vary depending on who is making them. This is especially true in controversial areas such as fisheries management, where the interests of many of the participants—fishing organizations, ocean conservation groups, and politicians—come into conflict.

Much of what is known about the oceans is really about ocean resources, since there is a great economic incentive to understand them. Besides being an enormous source of food, the oceans provide mineral and energy reserves, pharmaceuticals, and easy transport for goods. Shorelines are a favorite spot for development because of their beauty and the recreational opportunities they provide. Coastal ecosystems such as coral reefs and mangrove forests serve as nurseries for young marine animals, protect the coasts from storm damage, and filter pollutants.

But the oceans are in serious trouble as the cumulative effects of pollution, overharvesting, and habitat destruction take their toll. Unlike environmental problems on land, which are usually visible, much of the damage to the oceans is unseen: Oil leaks from underwater pipelines and offshore oil rigs; plastics wash up on distant shores and the inhabitants, if there are any, have no power to stop more from coming; marine animals accumulate toxins so that they fail to reproduce or die. We must monitor what is put into the sea and understand its effects.

Declines in fish populations due to overfishing are easier to see, but they are difficult to monitor and understand. Although anyone can observe that the seas are no longer thick with enormous numbers of fish as they were more than a century ago, no one alive then is around today to bear witness to the contrast. Even so, people who are just a few decades old can see the difference between the numbers of fish that were present during their childhoods and the numbers now. Getting real numbers on the decline is difficult, though, because not only does no one know how many fish there were in past decades, it is extremely difficult to get an accurate count today. As long as fish are coming out of the sea, many people will turn a blind eye to the long-term prognosis of fisheries.

In his 2003 book, *Heal the Ocean*, Dr. Rod Fujita describes the cycle of denial followed by crisis, in which fishers deny that a fishery is being depleted and continue to harvest from it, often while using ever more advanced technological equipment. Finally, when the fishery has nearly collapsed, it will be closed, but possibly too late for the fish population to recover. Furthermore, the decline or decimation of a fish species changes the dynamics of the entire ecosystem, causing starvation of other animals that rely on it for food.

For the sake of ecosystems and the people who rely on fishing for their livelihoods, fisheries should be managed for the long term;

they must be sustainable. The life cycles and habits of the target species need to be better understood as does their role in the ecosystem. Fishing techniques should be studied for the amount of bycatch they produce and for their impact on the whole environment. Banning drift nets was a positive step toward reducing bycatch; now it is necessary to ban or restrict bottom trawling so that additional habitat is not destroyed. It is imperative that fishers comply with regulations.

When fisheries decline, fishing communities suffer because jobs and revenue are lost. Therefore, fishers need to come together with scientists, environmentalists, and community leaders to develop solutions that work for their communities and that are acceptable to all groups. These leaders must develop plans that assure that the short-term needs of community members are met whenever possible even as long-term sustainability is being achieved.

As fish numbers fall off, the human population continues to grow, so there is need for more fish and seafood. Aquaculture is rapidly expanding to fill this gap. When poorly implemented, though, aquaculture jeopardizes native fish, pollutes the environment, and uses up limited resources, such as feed fish. Sound aquaculture practices, such as polyculture and organic farming, can make the difference between aquaculture that is a drain on the environment and aquaculture that is a benefit for both people and the planet.

Habitat destruction from ruinous fishing techniques, bad aquaculture practices, and coastal development destroys the ecosystem in which marine organisms live and drives their populations down. Habitat destruction also impairs the services that these ecosystems provide, such as coastal protection and pollutant filtering. To protect important habitats, development should be discouraged in sensitive regions, susceptible habitats should be protected, and damaged habitats should be restored where possible. Habitat restoration has begun in some areas, including the initiation of the largest wetlands restoration project ever attempted in the South San Francisco Bay. Despite these excellent efforts, it is easier to protect a natural habitat than to try to build a replacement; in other words, conservation of valuable habitats should always be the first choice.

Letting consumers know which products are fished or farmed sustainably and encouraging them to choose only those products will help drive seafood suppliers to use only environmentally sound practices. Information about the practices that brought a fish to market is found today at some specialty shops, but one hopes that more mainstream markets will soon provide this information. The example of "dolphin safe" tuna shows how consumers can bring about changes in fishing practices in both national and international fleets.

Marine reserves are needed to serve as a "bank" for species whose populations are in decline due to overfishing or habitat destruction. Reserves keep a portion of a habitat as pristine as possible, so that scientists have a model of what the environment should be like and to harbor a variety of native species. Experts suggest that 30% to 50% of the oceans should be off limits to fishing to help fisheries recover.

Coral reef ecosystems may be the most threatened because they are being attacked from an enormous number of directions. Each reef is faced with one or more different problems, ranging from destructive fishing practices to overfishing, excess sedimentation, harmful algal blooms, and even tourism. The greatest problem, however, comes from rising ocean temperatures, which are the primary cause of coral bleaching. Carbon dioxide, one of the primary greenhouse gases, increases the acidity of seawater, which is also a threat to corals and other shell-creating animals.

Climate change is likely the largest environmental concern the planet faces. Yet little is being done at this time to limit the release of greenhouse gases into the atmosphere, particularly in the United States, which is the largest emitter of these climate-altering substances (although it will soon be overtaken by China). Climate scientists have generated ideas that should be taken seriously by world governments, such as capping greenhouse gas emissions, developing alternative energy sources, and capturing carbon to store it in the ground. Although the problem of climate change is much more complex, people's success at reducing ozone depletion is a good example of how international cooperation can solve an environmental problem.

New problems will affect the oceans as countries extract resources that so far have been unutilized. Mineral resources, such as metals from hydrothermal vents or from manganese nodules, will be difficult to mine from the sea without causing environmental damage. The use of methane hydrates, potentially a tremendous source of energy, could bring about even more global warming. Before minerals and energy sources are utilized, their full impacts must be understood.

In developed nations, people consume ever more energy and materials as their lifestyles improve. While attempting to improve the standard of living of their inhabitants, developing nations are also increasing consumption. Consumption uses energy and material resources and produces pollutants. Inhabitants of developed nations should be offered incentives to consume environmentally friendly products and to develop technologies that improve energy efficiency and decrease waste. Developing economies should be encouraged to embrace technologies that are nonpolluting and renewable. Around the world, regulations must be enacted that protect the environment on both national and international levels. Pollution needs to be regulated, monitored, and decreased in all parts of the world.

The Pew Commission report says, "We have failed to conceive of the oceans as our largest public domain, to be managed holistically for the greater public good in perpetuity." The report concludes that what is needed is "an ethic of stewardship and responsibility toward the oceans. Most importantly, we must treat our oceans as a public trust."

Awareness of environmental issues is rising, at least in developed countries. Education is needed, not only in schools, but also within communities, to further the process. It is essential that everyone learn about the science behind the problems facing modern society and make informed decisions regarding lifestyle choices. Education should include the development of an environmental ethic that encourages, among other things, stewardship of the oceans. Individuals need to do what they can by reducing consumption and voting with their pocketbooks, buying only necessary and environmentally friendly (or at least less damaging) products. Perhaps most importantly, people must bring their knowledge of these topics to bear when making political decisions: to support candidates who are more likely to implement policies that value the long-term future of the planet and who will work toward the adoption of those policies in the United States and internationally.

Educated in the needs of the world and its environment and filled with hope and enthusiasm, young people will play a major role in implementing change. The path the world is taking can be turned around, incrementally and completely, with knowledge, dedication, and determination.

Glossary

abyssal plains Flat, featureless areas in the ocean floor in which any topography is covered over by abundant sediments.

acid A substance that produces hydrogen ions in solution.

adaptation A structure or behavior alteration that is inheritable; that is, able to be passed from one generation to the next.

aerobic Containing oxygen or requiring oxygen.

algae A very diverse group that make up a portion of two different kingdoms (Plantae and Protista); many are not plants, although all photosynthesize. Most are aquatic; most seaweeds are algae.

alkaline A solution in which hydroxyl ion is present in excess; alkaline solutions have numbers above 7 on the pH scale.

anaerobic Not containing oxygen or not requiring oxygen.

aphotic zone The dark portion of the ocean beneath the photic zone; most of the ocean is aphotic.

aquaculture The raising and harvesting of seaweed, fish, and shellfish in a water environment under controlled conditions.

arthropods Most of the planet's arthropods are insects. Marine arthropods include zooplankton, such as krill and copepods; crabs; lobsters; and shrimp.

atom The smallest unit of a chemical element having the properties of that element.

bacteria Microscopic single-celled organisms that live in an incredible number of environments.

barrier island A long, narrow strip of sand running parallel to the shore that protects inland areas from storms.

basalt A dark-colored, relatively dense volcanic rock formed of cooled lava that makes up the bulk of the seafloor.

bathymetric map A topographic map of the seafloor in which three-dimensional features are shown in two dimensions.

benthic Organisms that live on the sea bottom.

bioaccumulation The accumulation of toxic substances within living organisms.

biodegradable Waste that living organisms can decompose into harmless inorganic materials; however, in some cases, such as with plastics, this process can take hundreds of years.

biodiversity The number of species in a given habitat.

bioluminescence Light produced by a chemical reaction.

biomass The mass of all the living matter in a given area or volume of a habitat.

black smoker An extremely hot hydrothermal vent in which metallic minerals precipitate from the vent water, making the area look as if black smoke is billowing out.

breakwater A man-made structure built parallel to the beach that interrupts waves coming into shore.

buffer A solution that resists changes in pH.

bycatch Fish that are unwanted by fishers because they are too small or too low in value, or because the fisher is not licensed to catch them. About 25% of all marine creatures caught are bycatch.

calcium carbonate ($CaCO_3$) The composition of the rock limestone used by corals and other animals to make their shells.

cetaceans Marine mammals that include whales, dolphins, and porpoises.

chemosynthesis The creation of food energy by breaking down chemicals.

coast The shoreline, where the land meets the ocean.

consumer   An organism that feeds on other plants or animals for food energy.

continental crust   The rocky material of the continents.

continental margin   The edge of a continent that is submerged by seawater and is made of continental crust; it consists of the continental shelf and continental slope.

continental shelf   The gradually sloping drowned edge of a continent.

copepod   An arthropod zooplankton that is an important food source for larger animals.

coral bleaching   The process by which coral, ordinarily colorful, turns white due to the loss of their zooxanthellae; happens mostly in response to elevated ocean temperatures.

coral reef   A mass of calcium carbonate made from coral and other organisms that is the foundation of a rich ecosystem.

Coriolis effect   The tendency of a moving object to appear to move sideways due to the Earth's rotation; often used in describing the movement of ocean currents.

covalent bond   Strong chemical bond in which atoms share electrons.

crust   The outer rocky layer of the Earth; the two main types of crust are continental and oceanic.

crustacean   Mostly marine members of the phylum Arthropoda; crustaceans include lobsters, crabs, and shrimp.

DDT   A member of the group of pollutants known as POPs (persistent organic pollutants). DDT was a very effective insecticide but was withdrawn from production when its negative effects (and those of its breakdown products) on birds and mammals were realized.

dead zone   An ocean region that is hostile to most life, usually due to eutrophication.

decomposer   An organism that breaks down the body parts of dead organisms into nutrients that can be used by other plants and animals.

delta   Where a river meets the ocean; nutrients are abundant, and water grades ranging from fresh to saline create unique habitats for many forms of life.

density   Mass per unit volume.

deposit feeder   An invertebrate animal that eats sediment, digests the organic material, and excretes the waste.

detritus feeder   An invertebrate animal that eats dead plant matter that has been decomposed by bacteria.

dioxin   A toxic chemical (POP) that is a byproduct of the manufacture of other chemicals and has been shown to be hazardous to animals and possibly humans.

downwelling   The process by which dense water flows from the surface to the deep ocean, taking nutrients and gases with it.

dredge   An extremely strong rectangular bucket that scrapes rocks from the seafloor and returns them to the ship.

eastern boundary currents   Wide, shallow, slow currents on the eastern sides of gyres.

ecosystem   The interrelationships of the plants and animals of a region and the raw materials that they need to live.

echinoderm   A group of marine organisms that attach to the seafloor. The group includes sea stars, brittle stars, sea urchins, sand dollars, and sea cucumbers.

echolocation   The use of sounds of different frequency to determine the sizes and shapes of nearby objects, thereby creating a "picture" of the environment.

ectotherm   An animal whose body temperature is the same as its surrounding environment; also called "cold blooded."

electron   A negatively charged particle that orbits an atom's nucleus.

El Niño   A temporary warming of the Pacific Ocean that has implications for global weather patterns.

endangered species   An organism that is threatened with extinction.

endocrine disruptor   A compound that interrupts the functions of the endocrine system, often interfering with the sexual development or success of a species; most are estrogens or estrogen mimics.

endotherm An animal that uses food energy to fuel its body temperature, which remains nearly constant without being affected by the temperature of its environment; also called "warm blooded."

epifauna Benthic animals that live on the seafloor.

estrogen Female vertebrate sex hormones that trigger the development of the sex organs and control the reproductive cycle.

estuary The location where a river meets the sea so that there is great variability in salinity and a rich habitat for diverse organisms.

eutrophication The changes that occur in seawater when excessive nutrients are released, as commonly occurs during the depletion of oxygen by bacteria.

evolution Change through time. In science, evolution usually refers to organic evolution, which is the change in organisms through time by the process of natural selection.

Exclusive Economic Zone (EEZ) The zone extending 200 nautical miles (370 km) from a nation's shore; within its EEZ a country has sovereign rights to resources (living and nonliving), economic activity, and environmental protection.

filter feeder An invertebrate animal that pumps water through its body, straining out food particles from the water.

food chain A chain that takes food energy from producer to primary consumer to secondary consumer and so on, ending with decomposers.

food web Overlapping food chains that form a web that makes up the biological portion of an ecosystem.

fossil fuels Ancient plants that have decayed and been transformed into a useable fuel, especially coal and petroleum. These fuels are really just stored ancient sunshine.

gene The unit of inheritance that passes a trait from one generation to the next.

global warming Observed rise in average global temperature.

gravity corer A device dropped from a ship that uses its acceleration due to gravity to slice deeply into seafloor sediments.

grazer An organism that eats plants.

greenhouse gases Gases that absorb heat radiated from the Earth. They include carbon dioxide, methane, ozone, nitrous oxide, and chlorofluorocarbons.

groin A man-made barrier placed at a right angle to a beach that is designed to collect sand moving in to the beach and slow longshore transport of sand from the beach.

gyre Five large ocean currents that travel in a circle around major portions of the ocean basins. They rotate clockwise in the Northern Hemisphere and counterclockwise in the Southern.

habitat An environment in which an organism lives, with distinctive features such as climate, resource availability, predators, plus many others.

harmful algal bloom (HAB) A bloom of algae that is harmful to other ocean life because it is toxic or it disturbs the functioning of a type of organism.

hurricane Deadly tropical cyclone characterized by high storm surge, abundant rainfall, and intense winds.

hydrocarbon An organic compound composed of hydrogen and carbon; fossil fuels are hydrocarbons.

hydrogen bond A weak chemical bond in which the positive side of one polar molecule is attracted to the negative side of another polar molecule.

hydrologic cycle The cycling of water between Earth's atmosphere, oceans, and freshwater reservoirs such as glaciers, streams, lakes, and groundwater aquifers.

hydrothermal vent A hot spring on the seafloor, usually found along a mid-ocean ridge, where extremely hot water meets frigid seawater and precipitates metallic minerals.

hypoxic Water containing little or no free oxygen.

individual fish quotas (IFQ) A quota system in which the total fishing quota is divided into percentage shares among the fishers using the fishery.

infauna Benthic animals that live buried in the soft sediment or bore into the rocky bottom.

intertidal zone The coastal zone between the highest high tide and the lowest low tide, where nutrients and light are ordinarily abundant.

invasive species Organisms that are introduced by human activities into a location where they are not native; marine invasive species often travel in the ballast water of ships.

invertebrate An animal without a backbone.

ion An atom that has lost or gained an electron so that it has a positive or negative charge.

ionic bond Chemical bond in which one atom gives one or more electrons to another atom.

jellies Formerly known as jellyfish, jellies are not fish; they are free-swimming invertebrates with bell-shaped bodies and long tentacles.

jetty A man-made structure that protects the inlets in barrier islands by collecting sand on the upstream side of a longshore current.

krill Crustacean zooplankton that make up the greatest biomass of any multicellular creature on Earth; an important part of the diet of many marine organisms, particularly in the Antarctic.

La Niña The reverse of an El Niño, in which the surface of the Pacific Ocean off South America is especially cold.

lagoon A relatively shallow, narrow body of water cut off from the sea by a barrier island, coral reef, or other feature.

limiting factor A physical or biological factor (for example, a nutrient or light) that restricts the number of individuals of a species that can exist in a given area.

longshore current A current that moves parallel to the shoreline.

manganese nodules Rocks formed of metal oxides that precipitate from seawater around a nucleus and contain manganese, iron, nickel, copper, and other metals.

mangrove A flowering tree that grows in dense forests along tropical shorelines and has its roots submerged for part of the day; mangrove ecosystems perform many important environmental services.

mantle   The middle layer of the Earth, between the crust and the core, composed of hot, very dense rock.

marine protected areas (MPAs)   MPAs are ocean territories in which activities are restricted; they vary in size, shape, and level of protection. Unlike marine reserves, most MPAs allow some fishing.

mercury   The only metal that is liquid at room temperature. It is toxic in liquid form and also as a salt or an organic compound.

metabolism   The sum of all the biochemical processes necessary for life, including the building up or breaking down of complex organic molecules from simpler substances.

methane   A hydrocarbon gas (CH4) that is the major component of natural gas. Methane is also a natural component of the atmosphere and a greenhouse gas.

methane hydrate   Water molecules that contain a methane molecule inside; the methane from these hydrates is useable as fuel.

methyl mercury   Mercury that bacteria have altered into a toxic organic form.

mid-ocean ridge   A 36,000 mile (60,000 km) long line of volcanoes running through all three major oceans, and taking up one-third of the ocean floor.

molecule   The smallest unit of a compound that has all the properties of that compound.

mollusks   Invertebrates with an internal or external shell. Mollusks include clams, snails, abalones, limpets, octopuses, and squid.

mutation   A random change in a gene that may be beneficial, harmful, or neutral to the success of the individual and species.

natural selection   The mechanism that drives organic evolution. Natural processes affect the reproductive success of an organism, which steers the way a species will evolve.

neutrons   Uncharged subatomic particles found in an atom's nucleus.

nonrenewable resource   A resource that is not replenished on a time-scale that is useful to humans, so that when it is gone, there is no more; petroleum and many mineral resources are nonrenewable.

nucleus   The center of an atom, composed of protons and neutrons.

nutrients   Biologically important elements that are critical to growth or to building shells or bones; nitrates, phosphorus, carbonate, and silicate are some nutrients for marine organisms.

oceanic crust   The rocky material of the seafloor with the average composition of basalt.

overfishing   When more fish are being taken from a fishery than are necessary to replenish the fishery.

ozone hole   A "hole" in the ozone layer where ozone concentrations are diminished; usually refers to the Antarctic ozone hole.

pathogens   Microorganisms—primarily bacteria, viruses, parasites, and toxic algae—that cause disease.

PCBs (polychlorinated biphenyls)   Extremely stable, water-soluble, persistent organic pollutants that bioaccumulate and are found globally.

pelagic   Organisms that live entirely in the water.

pH   Numbers from 0 to 14 that express the acidity or alkalinity of a solution. On the pH scale, 7 is neutral, with lower numbers indicating acid and higher numbers indicating base. The most extreme numbers are the most extreme solutions.

photic zone   The thin surface layer of the ocean where light penetrates so that photosynthesis is possible.

photosynthesis   The process in which plants use carbon dioxide and water to produce sugar and oxygen. The simplified chemical reaction is $6CO_2 + 12H_2O + \text{solar energy} = C_6H_{12}O_6 + 6O_2 + 6H_2O$.

phytoplankton   Microscopic plantlike, usually single-celled organisms found at the surface of the ocean; they are the planet's single greatest source of oxygen.

pinniped   Meat-eating marine mammals that includes seals, sea lions, and walruses.

plankton   Tiny plants (phytoplankton) and animals (zooplankton) that live at the sea surface and form the lower levels of the ocean's food web.

plate tectonics   The theory that the Earth's surface is divided into plates that move on the planet's surface, driven by mantle convection.

polar molecule   A molecule in which one side has a positive charge and the other a negative charge; water is a polar molecule.

polychlorinated biphenyls   *See* **PCBs.**

polyculture   A method of aquaculture in which several species of animal are farmed together.

polyp   A small cup-shaped animal with a ring of tentacles, such as the coral polyp, that constructs a calcium carbonate structure around itself.

predator   An organism that kills and eats other animals for food energy.

primary productivity   The food energy created by producers.

producer   An organism that produces food energy from inorganic substances; usually used in reference to a plant that creates food energy via photosynthesis.

protons   Positively charged subatomic particles found in an atom's nucleus.

quota   A limit placed on a fishery, setting the number of a particular species that can be taken in a season.

remotely operated vehicle (ROV)   An unmanned submarine that remains tethered to the ship and transmits data in real time up a fiber-optic cable.

renewable resource   A resource that is replaced in a timescale such that it will not be depleted (within reason); tidal energy and salt are renewable resources.

respiration   The process by which an organism exchanges gases with the environment. In the reaction, sugar and CO_2 are converted into oxygen and water with the release of energy.

saline   Water containing salt.

scavenger   An animal that eats dead plants or animals for food energy.

sea   A landlocked or partially landlocked body of water.

seafloor spreading The mechanism for moving continents; the formation of new seafloor at spreading ridges pushes the plates on the Earth's surface outward.

seamount An ocean volcano that does not rise above sea level but is larger than an abyssal hill.

seawall A man-made barrier built along the edge of a shoreline to protect the land behind it from incoming waves.

sediment Fragments of rocks and minerals that range in size from dust and clay up to boulders.

sewage The waste matter that travels through sewers, including the material that leaves the drains of homes, businesses, and industries and that runs off the ground surface.

sewage sludge The material that remains after the water from sewage has evaporated.

solubility The ability of a substance to dissolve in a liquid.

solvent A liquid that is capable of dissolving (as with a solid) or dispersing (as with a liquid) another substance.

sonar (**SO**und **NA**vigation and **R**anging) Use of sound waves by humans and some marine mammals to determine distance and shape of an object in the sea.

species A classification of organisms that includes those that can or do interbreed and produce fertile offspring; members of a species share the same gene pool.

sponge Primitive, invertebrate, aquatic, filter-feeding animals that live attached to the seafloor.

storm surge Local sea level rise caused by high winds blowing ocean water onto a shoreline during a storm.

subduction The plate tectonics process in which seafloor plunges into the mantle and recycles older oceanic crust.

submersible A small, manned submarine that travels beneath the sea surface and is not tethered to the mother ship.

surface tension The attraction of molecules to one another on a liquid's surface; water's high surface tension causes the liquid to form drops and allows insects to land on it.

symbiosis A relationship in which organisms from different species habitually live together, usually to the benefit of both species.

theory An explanation for a natural phenomenon that is supported by virtually all data and has no inconsistencies. It may be used to predict future events.

threatened species A species that is likely to become endangered in the future.

tide The regular rise and fall of sea level (or lake level) due to the gravitational attraction of the Moon and Sun to Earth.

trench Long, narrow, and deep valleys that form at subduction zones.

tributyltin (TBT) A tin-containing compound that is an effective anti-fouling agent and an endocrine disruptor.

tsunami Catastrophic ocean waves caused by a shock to the seafloor or sea surface, usually an earthquake.

ultraviolet radiation (UV) Shortwave, high energy solar radiation; the highest energy wavelengths of UV are extremely harmful to life.

upwelling Upward flow of lower density water from the deep ocean to the sea surface.

vertebrate An animal with a backbone; fish, amphibians, reptiles, birds, and mammals are all vertebrates.

water vapor Water (H_2O) in its gaseous state.

western boundary current Swift, deep, narrow currents on the western sides of gyres; the Gulf Stream is a western boundary current.

zooplankton Animal plankton that are unable to swim on their own and that drift with the currents. Most are tiny; some are the larvae of benthic organisms.

zooxanthellae Single-celled dinoflagellates (algae) that live in a symbiotic relationship with corals; the zooxanthellae supply oxygen and food to the corals and the corals supply a home and nutrients (their wastes) for the algae.

Further Reading

Burdick, Alan. *Out of Eden: An Odyssey of Ecological Invasion.* New York: Farrar, Straus and Giroux, 2005.

Dean, Cornelia. *Against the Tide: The Battle for America's Beaches.* New York: Columbia University Press, 1999.

———. "From the Air, Scientists Comb a Ruined Coastline for Clues and Lessons." *The New York Times*, September 6, 2005.

Fujita, Rod. *Heal the Ocean: Solutions for Saving Our Seas.* Gabriola Island, Canada: New Society Publishers, 2003.

Lovgren, Stefan. "Exxon Valdez Spill, 15 Years Later: Damage Lingers." *National Geographic News* (March 2004). Available online. URL: http://news.nationalgeographic.com/news/2004/03/0318_040318_exxonvaldez.html. Accessed March 8, 2007.

Mastny, Lisa. "Healthy Coastlines Mitigate Disasters." *World Watch* 18 (May/June 2005): p. 7

Moore, Charles. "Trashed: Across the Pacific Ocean, Plastics, Plastics, Everywhere." *Natural History* 11 (November 2003): pp. 46–52.

National Oceanic and Atmospheric Administration (NOAA). "Coral Reef Home Page." Available online. URL: http://www.publicaffairs.noaa.gov/coral-reef.html. Accessed March 8, 2007.

———. "25 Things You Can Do to Save Coral Reefs." Available online. URL: http://www.publicaffairs.noaa.gov/25list.html. Accessed March 8, 2007.

Public Broadcasting Service (PBS). "Secrets of the Ocean Realm." Available online. URL: http://www.pbs.org/oceanrealm/index.html. Accessed March 8, 2007.

Roach, John. "Cousteau Finds 'Horrifying' Trash on Desert Islands." *National Geographic News* (July 2003). Available online. URL: http://

news.nationalgeographic.com/news/2003/07/0728_030728_trashha-waii.html. Accessed March 8, 2007.

Safina, Carl. *Song for the Blue Ocean: Encounters Along the World's Coasts and Beneath the Seas.* New York: Henry Holt and Company, 1997.

———, Andrew A. Rosenberg, Ransom A. Myers, Terrance J. Quinn II, and Jeremy S. Collie. "U.S. Ocean Fish Recovery: Staying the Course." *Science* 309 (July 2005): pp. 707–708.

"South Bay Challenge: Reclaiming the Salt Ponds for People and Nature." SouthBayRestoration.org (2004). Available online. URL: http://www.southbayrestoration.org/pdf_files/BayNature%20Oct%202004.pdf. Accessed March 8, 2007.

Van Dover, Cindy Lee. *The Octopus's Garden: Hydrothermal Vents and Other Mysteries of the Deep Sea.* Boston: Addison Wesley, 1996.

"United Nations Convention on the Law of the Sea." Available online. URL: http://www.un.org/Depts/los/convention_agreements/convention_historical_perspective.htm#Historical%20Perspective. Accessed March 8, 2007.

Wilkinson, Clive. *Status of Coral Reefs of the World: 2004.* Australian Institute of Marine Science (2004). Available online. URL: http://www.aims.gov.au/pages/research/coral-bleaching/scr2004/. Accessed March 8, 2007.

Web Sites

Blue Ocean Institute
http://www.blueocean.org
Carl Safina's ocean conservation group includes an ocean friendly seafood list.

Cetacea
http://www.cetacea.org/index.htm
Complete information on every species of whale, dolphin, and porpoise.

Chesapeake Bay Program
http://www.chesapeakebay.net
The current state of the Chesapeake Bay ecosystem and the work being done to restore it to a more natural system.

Deep Ocean Exploration Institute

http://www.whoi.edu/page.do?pid-7400

*Current topics in deep ocean exploration from the Woods Hole
    Oceanographic Institution.*

Environmental Defense Oceans Alive

http://www.oceansalive.org/eat.cfm?sitecode=edhp2

*The Environmental Defense list of good and bad seafood choices
    includes health information.*

Harmful Algae Page

http://www.whoi.edu/redtide/

*All about the causes and effects of harmful algae from the Woods Hole
    Oceanic Institution.*

Mangroves

http://www.nhmi.org/mangroves/index.htm

*Basic information about the physiology, reproduction, and ecology of
    mangroves from the Seacamp Association.*

Monterey Bay Aquarium's Seafood Watch

http://www.montereybayaquarium.org/cr/seafoodwatch.asp

Includes regional guides to environmentally sound seafood choices.

**National Marine Fisheries Service (NMFS), National Oceanic and
    Atmospheric Administration (NOAA)**

http://www.nmfs.noaa.gov

*This branch of NOAA provides information on fishing techniques,
    sustainable fishing practices, strandings, and other topics in
    fisheries management.*

**National Marine Sanctuaries, National Oceanic and Atmospheric
    Administration (NOAA)**

http://www.sanctuaries.nos.noaa.gov/welcome.html

Information on marine sanctuaries within the United States.

National Oceanic and Atmospheric Administration (NOAA)

http://www.noaa.gov

*The NOAA Web site contains an enormous amount of scientific
information on weather, climate, oceans, coasts, global change,
and other current topics.*

Oceanus

http://www.whoi.edu/oceanus/index.do

The journal Oceanus *provides access to many current research topics
being pursued by scientists at the Woods Hole Oceanographic
Institution.*

Science Daily

http://www.sciencedaily.com

*An online site for current science news in all topics, including
oceanography and the environment.*

Sea Otter Research

http://www.seaotterresearch.org

*Current research on California sea otters from the University of
California, Davis.*

SeaWeb

http://www.seaweb.org

*SeaWeb is a project designed to raise awareness of the world's oceans
and the life within them.*

South Bay Salt Pond Restoration Project

http://www.southbayrestoration.org/index.html

*Web site for the South Bay Salt Pond Restoration Project: the
largest tidal wetland restoration project on the West Coast of the
United States.*

Vents Program, National Oceanic and Atmospheric Administration
http://www.pmel.noaa.gov/vents/index.html#
Research on underwater hydrothermal venting systems.

Virginia Institute of Marine Science
http://www.vims.edu/env/projects/pfiesteria/index.html
Current Pfiesteria research at the Virginia Institute of Marine Science.

Index

About the Author

DANA DESONIE, Ph.D., has written about the earth, ocean, space, life, and environmental sciences for more than a decade. Her work has appeared in educational lessons, textbooks, and magazines, and on radio and the Web. Her 1996 book, *Cosmic Collisions*, described the importance of asteroids and comets in Earth history and the possible consequences of a future asteroid collision with the planet. Before becoming a science writer, she received a doctorate in oceanography, spending weeks at a time at sea, mostly in the tropics, and one amazing day at the bottom of the Pacific in the research submersible *Alvin* (piloted by Dr. Cindy Lee Van Dover). She now resides in Phoenix, Arizona, with her neuroscientist husband, Miles Orchinik, and their two children.